God and Me!®

RoseKidz®
An imprint of Hendrickson Publishers Marketing, LLC.
Peabody, Massachusetts
www.HendricksonRose.com

Devotions for Girls Ages 6-9

God and Me!®

by Diane Cory

To my mother, Mary, for praying for me during the writing of this book.
Also, to my friend in children's ministry, Lori Turner, for the many hours she spent proofreading this work and encouraging me.

God and Me!® for Ages 6-9

RoseKidz®
An imprint of Hendrickson Publishers Marketing, LLC.
P. O. Box 3473, Peabody
Massachusetts 01961-3473
www.HendricksonRose.com

Register your book at www. HendricksonRose.com/register and receive a free Bible Reference download.

Cover Illustrator: Chuck Galey
Interior Illustrator: Aline L. Heiser

ISBN10: 1-885358-60-1
ISBN13: 978-1-885358-60-8
RoseKidz #L46822
Juvenile Nonfiction/Religion/Devotion & Prayer

Printed in the United States of America [37] 05.2017.VP

Table of Contents

Table of Contents

Table of Contents

Introduction

Did you know that God wants to be your very special friend? He knows everything about you but He wants you to know Him. This book will help you know God and His ways. You will learn about God's love for you. You will also learn He loves all people.

Learning to live God's way isn't always easy. But living God's way is different than living your own way. It means to love God and obey Him even when you don't want to. Living His way is the only way to be happy.

Share this page with your parents. Ask them to help you with words in this book that you do not understand. If you are just learning to read, let a parent read this book with you.

Here are steps to use God and Me!:

1. Read the devotion name and the purpose.
2. Read the Bible verse. Look it up in your Bible. Draw a line under the words in your Bible to help you quickly find the verse later. God doesn't mind if you draw a neat line in His words.
3. Read the story or have your parents read it to you. Answer the questions.
4. Think about the answers to the questions. Pray to God. Talk to Him about what you have learned. Try to spend a minute or more just listening for God's voice in your heart and mind.
5. Read the activity directions and do the activity. The projects and puzzles will help you act on what you learn.

Use this book each day in a special time alone with God. Take time to talk to God in prayer as you go through this book. Have fun loving God and learning about Him every day!

Who Is God?

God's Word

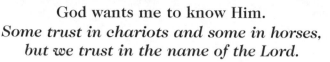

God wants me to know Him.
Some trust in chariots and some in horses,
but we trust in the name of the Lord.

Psalm 20:7

God Shows Himself in the Bible

"What's your name?"

"My name is Sally. I live in the yellow house on the corner."

"It's nice to meet you, Sally. My name is Tracy. I live in the blue house by the park."

When you meet someone it is good to know her name. How do you explain to others who you are? If you tell them your name, you share one of the most important things about you. By trading names with others, you are telling about yourself. God tells about Himself in the Bible. Isaiah 42:8 says, "I am the Lord; that is my name!" God wants you to know Him as well as you know your family members. He already knows everything about you. Matthew 10:30 says, "Even the very hairs of your head are all numbered."

Your Turn

1. How can you explain to others who you are?
2. How does God tell you who He is?
3. How can you tell others about God?

Prayer

Thank You, God, that I can meet new people. Teach me to tell others about You. Amen.

The Address Book

Fill out the address book on this page. Write the names of friends and family in the address book. Pray for each person every day.

God's Word

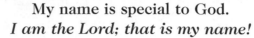

My name is special to God.

I am the Lord; that is my name!

Isaiah 42:8

Every Name Tells a Story

Sally Joy Kramer.

Ann Marie Smith.

Most people have a first, middle and last name. Every name tells something. The person who named you had a reason for giving you your name. Your name has meaning.

Some people in the Old Testament of the Bible were called Hebrews. The Hebrews were God's first people. Each Hebrew child had a name that told something about her. The name was the greatness hoped for in that child. For example, Sarah means "princess." She became a very beautiful woman inside and outside. Her parents hoped she would be a princess for God when they named her Sarah. Noah means "comforter." Noah's parents hoped he would comfort people who were sad.

A name tells what a person is like and who they are. What story does your name tell? Look for the meaning of your name in a name book.

Your Turn

1. How did your parents choose your name? Look up the story of your name in a book of names. Ask your parents how you got your name.
2. Tell a friend your middle name.
3. Why do you think God wants you to know His name?

Prayer

Thank You, God, for my name. Teach me more about Your name, God. I want to know You. I want to tell others about You. Amen.

Name Squares Puzzle

Write your name going down the squares. Place each letter in your name in a square. Make new boxes if you need to. Use the letters in your name to make new words across that tell about you.

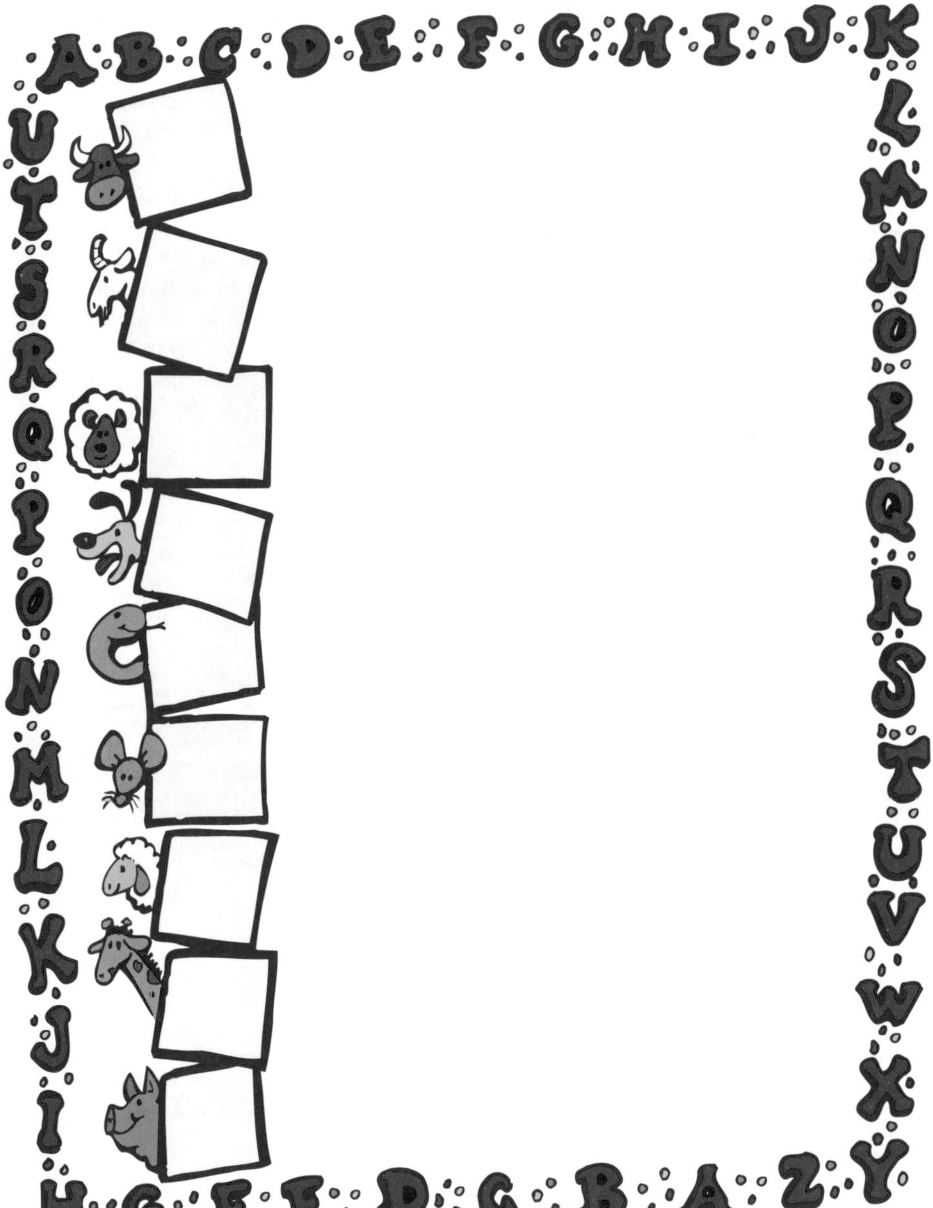

God's Word

I can learn about God from the Bible.
Our help is in the name of the Lord.
Psalm 124:8

The Bible Tells What God Is Like

The day you were born was a happy day for your parents. Before you came home from the hospital, they signed birth papers. A birth paper tells all about you. It tells your name. It tells your parents' names. It also tells the time and place you were born.

Did you know that there is no way of knowing God's age? No one knows when or where He was born. God has always been here. God doesn't have parents. You can show your birth papers to someone to prove who you are and to prove where and when you were born. God does not need a birth paper. He has shown us who He is in the Bible.

The Bible tells what God is like. The Bible is like birth papers for God. The Bible tells what God does. It tells that He is the Creator. He is the God who sees, the God who is always there, and the Shepherd. The Bible also says that He is the all-sufficient One, never-changing Jehovah, and Immanuel, or "God with us."

Your Turn

1. How can the Bible be a birth paper for God?
2. Why do you want to know who God is?

Prayer

I thank You, God, for the Bible. The Bible tells us who You are and what You are like. Teach me to read Your word each day. Amen.

God's Birth Papers

Look at your birth papers and baby book. Share the facts about yourself with your class or a friend. Then fill out the birth papers below for God. In the space for God's name write words about God. For example: "good," "loving" or "kind." Write "unknown" in the space for place of birth and time of birth.

Certificate of Birth

Name: First ______ *Middle* ______ *Last* ______

Girl/Boy ______ *Date of Birth* ______ *Hour of Birth* ______

Hospital Name ______ *City/Town* ______

Doctor's Name ______

Mother's Name: First ______ *Middle* ______ *Maiden* ______

Father's Name: First ______ *Middle* ______ *Last* ______

God, the Creator

God knew all about me when He created the earth.
But be glad and rejoice forever in what I will create.
Isaiah 65:18

God's Plans for My Life

Did you ever make plans to do something important? Are you planning for a birthday party or a camping trip with your mom or dad?

God made plans for you before you were born. God made the heavens and the earth. He planned to make a place for you to live and grow. God loved you then, and He loves you now.

Imagine, God knew about you while He created the earth. He prepared a place with air, water and land. God made good plans for you to live.

Can you be glad and rejoice in all God has created? Thank Him now for all He made for you to live. You can read about God creating the heavens and the earth in Genesis 1:6-8.

Your Turn

1. How can you hear about God's plans for your life?
2. How can you help your friends know that God has a plan for their lives?

Prayer

Thank You, God, for making plans to care for me. Thank You for the air I breathe. Help me to follow Your plans for me. Amen.

Making Plans

Create a plan to spend time with a person soon. Make an invitation below explaining the plan you created. God planned long ago to spend time with you now. God's invitation to you is found in the Bible.

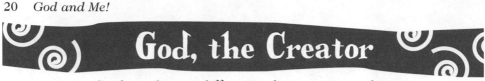

God, the Creator

God made me different than anyone else.

God created man in his own image...
male and female He created them.

Genesis 1:27

Someone Like You

Did you know there is someone like you? Maybe you have your mother's eye color. Perhaps you have your grandfather's hair color. Your nose may be shaped like the nose of an uncle or aunt. Do you laugh like your brother? All family members have things about them they share. Can you think of certain ways you are like other family members?

God created people to be like Him in special ways. God can smell! Do you have a nose? God can speak! Do you have a mouth? God can see! Do you have eyes? God can hear! Do you have ears?

We don't know what God looks like. God doesn't need to have a body to have a nose, mouth, eyes or ears. God made your body to do what He does without a body. God is the one who made you different than anyone. In Genesis 1:26-28 you can read about how God created people in His image.

Your Turn

1. Why did God create you?
2. Whom do you look like in your family?
3. How are you like God? Can you see how you are made in the image of God?

____

____

____

____

____

____

____

____

Prayer

Thank You, God, for my life and for creating me. Amen.

Family Art

Draw a picture or take a snapshot of a family member's nose, ears, mouth, etc. Glue the picture in the frame. Ask your mother, father or grandparents to share some family picture albums with you.

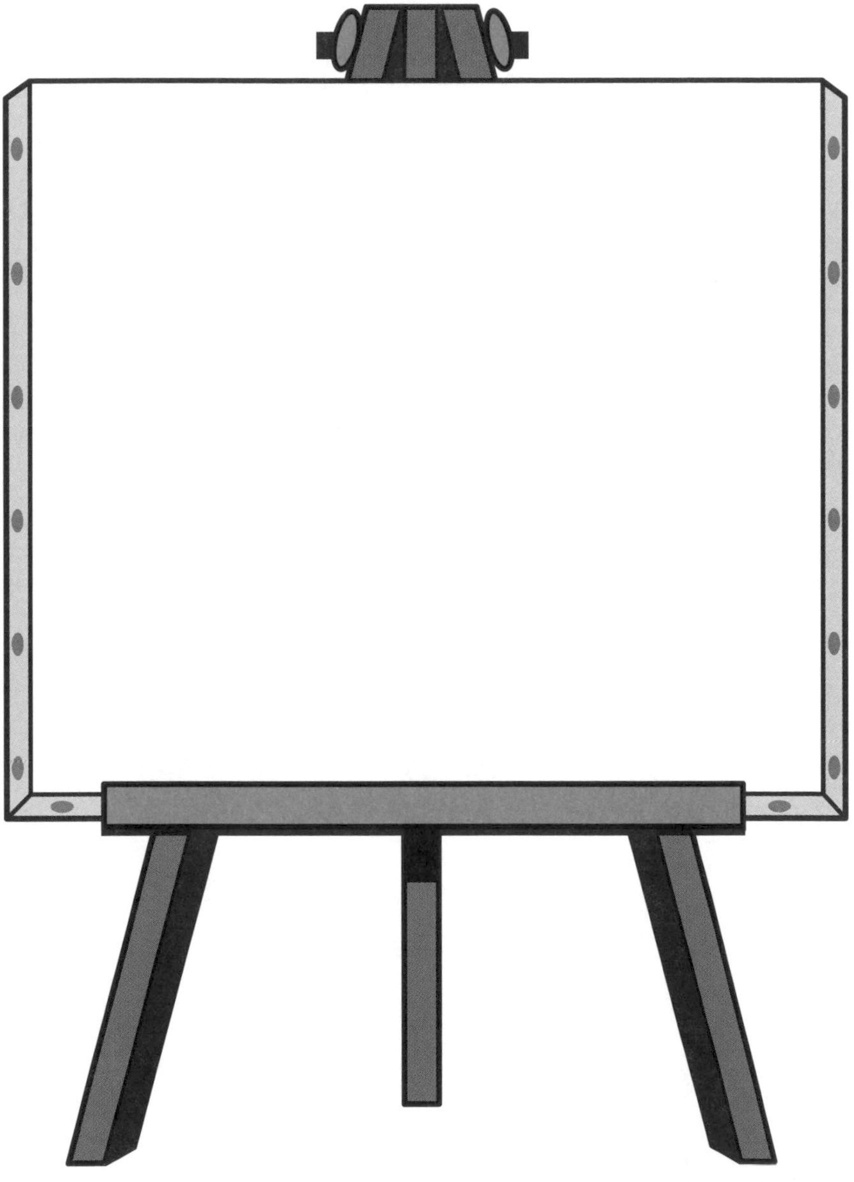

God, the Creator

God used His power to create animals.

He did not create [the earth] to be empty, but formed it to be inhabited [filled].

Isaiah 45:18

God's Animals

Do you have a pet that you love? Do you have a friend who has a pet? God also has pets. He created many different kinds of animals.

When God created the world, He prepared it for animals and people. God made ocean beds swarm with different shapes and sizes of fish. Birds came to life and covered the sky.

On the sixth day of Creation, God made land animals. The Bible says that some animals were tame. Others were wild. He created animals that crawl on the ground — God used His power to create the smallest ladybug. His power once created the largest dinosaur.

God lovingly spoke a blessing on each animal. God even talked to the animals. He told them to grow in their numbers. Read about God creating the animals in Genesis 1:20-25.

Your Turn

1. Can you name some of the animals in the Bible?
2. Why do you think God created animals?
3. Look up your favorite animal in an encyclopedia. Tell your mom or dad about it.

Prayer

Thank You, God, for creating animals. Thank You for my pet. Amen.

God's Farm

Read Job 40:15-20. Find "behemoth" in a dictionary. Could that be a dinosaur? Draw pictures below of some animals in the Bible and label them with their Bible reference from the Creation story in Genesis.

God, the Creator

God created the moon for a night light.

He...calls them each by name.

Psalm 147:4

The Night and Day Sky

Could you see yourself as an astronaut on a rocket? Imagine that you are the first girl on the moon. You would see a lot of stars there, wouldn't you? On a clear night, you can see a star lit sky even from earth. It looks like there are hundreds of stars hanging in space!

There are more stars in space than you can count. Yet God named every star. God created a special star for earth. Do you know that star? It is the sun! We need light to do our work, read books and play games. The moon was created to be our night light. God calls the moon the lesser light in Genesis 1:16. Find out more about the sky in Genesis 1:14-19.

Your Turn

1. Why did God create light?
2. Why do you think God made the stars so far away?
3. Do you know any star stories from the Bible (hint: star of Bethlehem)?

Prayer

God, I see Your work in the night sky. Thank You for being my God. Amen.

Naming the Stars

Add your own stars to the stars on this page. Pretend you are helping God name the stars. Make up star names. Check the library for books on the stars. Read about God's star creations!

God, the Creator

God wants me to enjoy His creations.

He makes grass grow for the cattle, and plants for man.

Psalm 104:14

God's Plants

A seed is the start of a plant. Plants, flowers, trees and grass begin as seeds. The grass on your lawn grew by someone planting grass seed. The tomato plants in your garden began as tomato seeds. Apple trees grow when an apple seed is planted.

Colorful flowers were created for you to see and enjoy. You can enjoy God's beautiful flowers planted in your yard. You can enjoy flowers and plants at weddings and parties.

God created all plant life. God didn't need to plant seeds to grow plants. He spoke and the tall trees appeared. He spoke again and colorful flowers showed blooms. He wants you to enjoy eating the fruits and vegetables He created.

God can create anything at anytime. Read about how God made the plants in Genesis 1:11-13.

Your Turn

1. Why does God create plants for you to enjoy?
2. How can you show God you are thankful for His plant creations?
3. What part of God's plant creations do you enjoy?

____

____

____

____

____

____

____

____

Prayer

God, thank You for all Your creations. I enjoy playing outside where I can see the plants You created. Amen.

Family Apple Tree

Write the names or faces of family members on the apples. Put your mother's family on one side of the tree. Put your father's family on the other side of the tree. Let this family apple tree remind you of God. The same God who created apple trees also created families!

The God Who Sees

God sees things I can't see.
You are the God who sees me.
Genesis 16:13

God Sees Things You Can't See

Do you know people who wear glasses to see better? Road signs look dim to those who forget to wear their glasses.

God never needs glasses to see. He is the God who sees everything.

Can you see a movie and your grandmother at the same time? God can!

Stand on the shore of a lake. Look down into the water. Can you see fish swimming at the bottom? God can!

God sees things you can't see. God sees things you will never see.

Your Turn

1. When God looks at you, what does He see?
2. What do you want God to see in your life?
3. What do you want to ask God to help you with?

Prayer

Lord, I love You. Please see me and let me know You. Help me when You see I am headed for trouble. Amen.

The Giant Eyeglasses

Draw a picture of yourself in one lens. Draw a picture of your family in the other lens. Remember, God lovingly sees you and your family. Another idea: play a travel car game when you go somewhere. Point to the things that God sees. Say, "God sees the trees," "God sees the birds," etc.

The God Who Sees

I can't see God but He sees me.

O Lord, you have searched me and you know me.

Psalm 139:1

I Can't See You, God

Saying good-bye to a friend or family member isn't easy. Jody recalls the day she watched her grandparents get onto an airplane. They flew back to their home after her eighth birthday party. She watched the plane travel down the runway. It flew into the sky and out of her sight. Jody couldn't see her grandma and grandpa face-to-face anymore. She knew they were on the plane, but she couldn't see them.

"I miss seeing them already," sighed Jody to her mother.

"We can call them tonight," her mother said.

"OK, at least I can talk to them," replied Jody.

Jody felt good knowing she could talk to her grandparents. You can't see God, but He sees you. Not seeing God doesn't keep you from knowing Him. You can talk to Him in prayer anytime.

Your Turn

1. Think of things God sees that you can't. Name a few.
2. What would you want God to show you if you could see anything?

Prayer

Please help me know You, God. Thank You for watching over me. Amen.

Eye Match

On the left side of the page there are faces showing four different feelings. On the right side of the page there are eyes for God. God knows how you feel. You can see your feelings in His eyes, just like these eyes show. Match your feeling on the left with the feelings in God's eyes on the right by drawing lines. The answers are on page 232.

The God Who Sees

God sees me, so He can help me.
You know when I sit and when I rise; you perceive my thoughts from afar.
Psalm 139:2

God Sees Me

Did you ever miss school due to a cold, chicken pox or the flu? You knew your teacher and the other kids were in the classroom at school. You could not see them, but they were there.

That is the way God is. You cannot see Him like you see family, friends, teachers or classmates. Yet you know He is there to see you. God sees you and knows everything about you. He sees you sit in your chair. He sees you comb your hair. He sees you kick your legs high in the swing. He sees how well you perform at ballet class. He sees you because He wants to help you. And He does.

Your Turn

1. Why does God keep His eyes on you?
2. You know God is watching. Does that change what you do?
3. You can't see God. How do you know He sees you?

Prayer

Thank You, God, for watching me and loving me. Amen.

My Psalm to God

Read Psalm 139:2 again. A psalm is like a song for God. Write your own psalm below by adding your words to each verse.

My Psalm to God

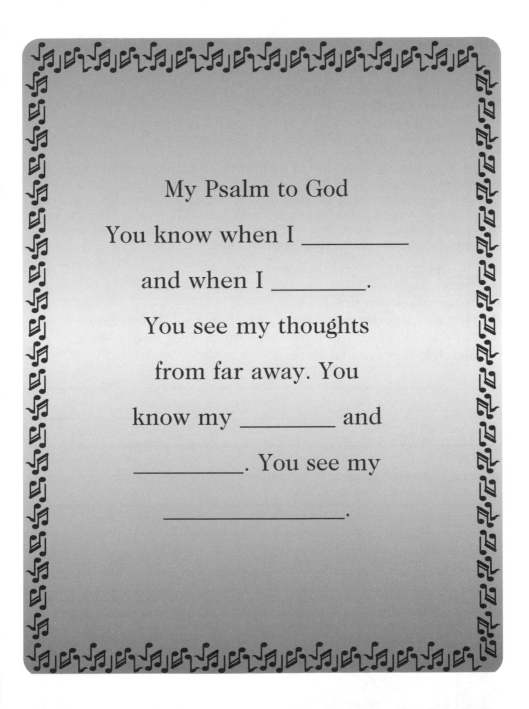

You know when I __________

and when I ________.

You see my thoughts

from far away. You

know my ________ and

__________. You see my

_________________.

The God Who Sees

God cares about my feelings.
Love one another deeply, from the heart.
1 Peter 1:22

God Cares About My Feelings

Do you live in an apartment or a house? The place you live is your home. Your home is where you stay.

A heart is like a home for your feelings. A heart is a place where your feelings are. Love and hate both live in your heart's home. A hug can make your heart home feel happy. A clap of thunder can make your heart home afraid. Your sister playing in your room without asking can make your heart home mad.

God sees everything in your heart home. He looks in your heart because He loves you. God wants to cheer you when you are sad. He wants to rejoice with you when you are happy. God will comfort you when you are afraid. He cares about all of your feelings.

Your Turn

1. What makes you afraid?
2. God sees you when you are afraid. How does He help you?
3. Do you think God can see feelings inside your heart? Name feelings you have that He sees.

Prayer

God, see inside my heart. When I am afraid, happy or sad, I know I can turn to You for help and comfort. Amen.

A Heart List

Tell God your heart feelings by making a list of your feelings inside the heart house below.

The God Who Sees

God sees inside my heart.

God is testing you to find out whether you love him with all your heart.

Deuteronomy 13:3

God's Flag Test

Flags fly to show how people feel about their country, state or favorite team. Each flag has colors or pictures on it to tell what the flag means. When people fly a flag you know they feel good about what the flag shows. There is a Christian flag with a cross that stands for Jesus dying on the cross for your sin. There is a Bible flag that shows that the Bible is a very important book.

God wants you to fly a pretend flag in your heart that says you love Him. Everyone should see your heart flag flying and know you love God.

Can you feel your heart beat with your hand when you pledge to the flag? Stethoscopes are used by doctors to see how many times your heart beats each minute. God doesn't test your heart with a stethoscope. God is greater than any doctor who hears or feels a beating heart. God can see inside and outside your heart to test it. His test is not to learn how many times it beats. God tests your heart to see if you love Him. Your heart is important to God because your feelings are there.

The heart is where you can show your flag of love for God. God sees the heart to find out if you really do love Him. Do you fly a heart flag of love for God?

Your Turn

1. How does God know if your heart really loves Him?
2. What would you act like if your heart truly loved God?
3. How can you tell if someone really loves God?

Prayer

God, I want to love You more. I want You to see my love for You in my heart and in my actions. Let my heart flag fly high for You. Amen.

My Flag for God

If you were going to fly a flag to let people know you love God, what would it look like? Make a heart flag of love for God on the flag pole below. Decorate it so people know you love God.

The God Who Sees

God sees everything I do.
"Can anyone hide in secret places so that I cannot see him?" declares the Lord.

Jeremiah 23:24

Hiding from God

One person puts her hands over her eyes while another person runs away and hides. The person counting stops and tries to find where the other person is hiding. What is the name of this game? Hide and Seek! Do you think you can hide from God?

Jonah, a man in the Bible, tried to hide from God. God followed Jonah everywhere he went. Jonah was a prophet whom God called to go and preach in a city named Nineveh. Jonah did not know that God is a God who sees. Jonah thought he could run and hide rather than obey God. Jonah was very wrong.

Stealing a snack from the kitchen is "doing a Jonah." Sneaking money from your mother's purse or lying are all Jonahs. You may think that no one is watching you, but God sees everything.

Your Turn

1. Can you think of a time or place when you have "pulled a Jonah"?
2. Share your memory with God. Ask God to forgive you. If you were mean to a person, ask him or her to forgive you.
3. Is there any place you can go or anything you can do where God cannot see you?

Prayer

Dear God, help me to obey You in everything I do and say. Let me know when I am pulling a Jonah. Amen.

My Daily Diary

At the end of each day, write down the things God saw you do that day.

Jehovah

Things may change, but God never changes.

Jesus Christ is the same yesterday and today and forever.

Hebrews 13:8

God Never Changes, Part One

Spring, summer, fall and winter! The seasons always bring change. School starts in the fall. The leaves on the trees change color and fall to the ground.

Winter winds bring cold and snow. There is a chill in the air. Ice skating and sledding begin.

Next, spring brings buds to the tips of the tree limbs.

Summer is all about swimming and in-line skating. Green leaves and butterflies show up in the summer.

Things around you may change, but God never changes.

Your Turn

1. Look outside and name the changes taking place around you right now.
2. How does God show you He never changes?
3. How can you help others to see that God never changes?

Prayer

God, thank You that Your love for me never changes. Amen.

Seasons Maze

Draw a line following the girl in-line skating through the seasons. Write at the bottom of the page how you have changed each time a season has changed. (Example: My hair is longer from fall to winter.)

Jehovah

I will change, but God is the same.

But you remain the same, and your years will never end.

Psalm 102:27

God Never Changes, Part 2

Step into the time machine! Close the door and set the dial for five years from now. What would you look like when you step out of the machine? A time machine can take you through time and not change you. Only time changes in a time machine.

God must have His own time machine because He never changes. Do you stay the same age? Will you be the same age in a year? Will you be the same size in two years? Will you always like the same food and movies?

God is the never-changing God, "Jehovah!" A time machine is not real. God is real. God never changes!

Your Turn

1. When would you like to go in a time machine?
2. What would you like to change about yourself?
3. What do you think God would like for you to change about yourself?

Prayer

I'm so glad You never change, God. Help me to change the things in me that make You sad, Lord. Amen.

The Time Machine Puzzle

Decode the secret message in the time machine. The answers are on page 232.

Jehovah

God works to help me.

Every good and perfect gift is from above, coming down from the Father of the heavenly lights, who does not change like shifting shadows.

James 1:17

The Gift Box

What would you like to be when you grow up? What is your father's job? What is your mother's job? Is your father a farmer or a policeman? Maybe your mother is a dentist or homemaker. Your parents come home after a day at work.

Your parents probably work a lot to take care of you, but God is always at work.

Did you know that God holds many jobs? God is a creator. God is a watchman. He cares for you like a shepherd cares for his sheep. God provides for you. He is there to give you what you need.

God gives each of these care jobs to you. Your parents work their jobs to care for you. God works His jobs as a gift of love to you. He doesn't want to be paid for His work. God's jobs are a gift.

Your Turn

1. God does many jobs as a gift to you. What jobs can you do for Him?
2. What jobs can you do as a gift to others?
3. Why would God give so many gifts of care?

Prayer

God, thank You for loving me enough to do what You do as a gift to me. You are an awesome God! Amen.

The Gift Box

Make a list of heart jobs that you can give to God in the gift box below. For example: worship, praise, love or obey. Draw a bow around the box. Save this gift list of heart jobs for Christmas. Put it under your Christmas tree as a gift to baby Jesus.

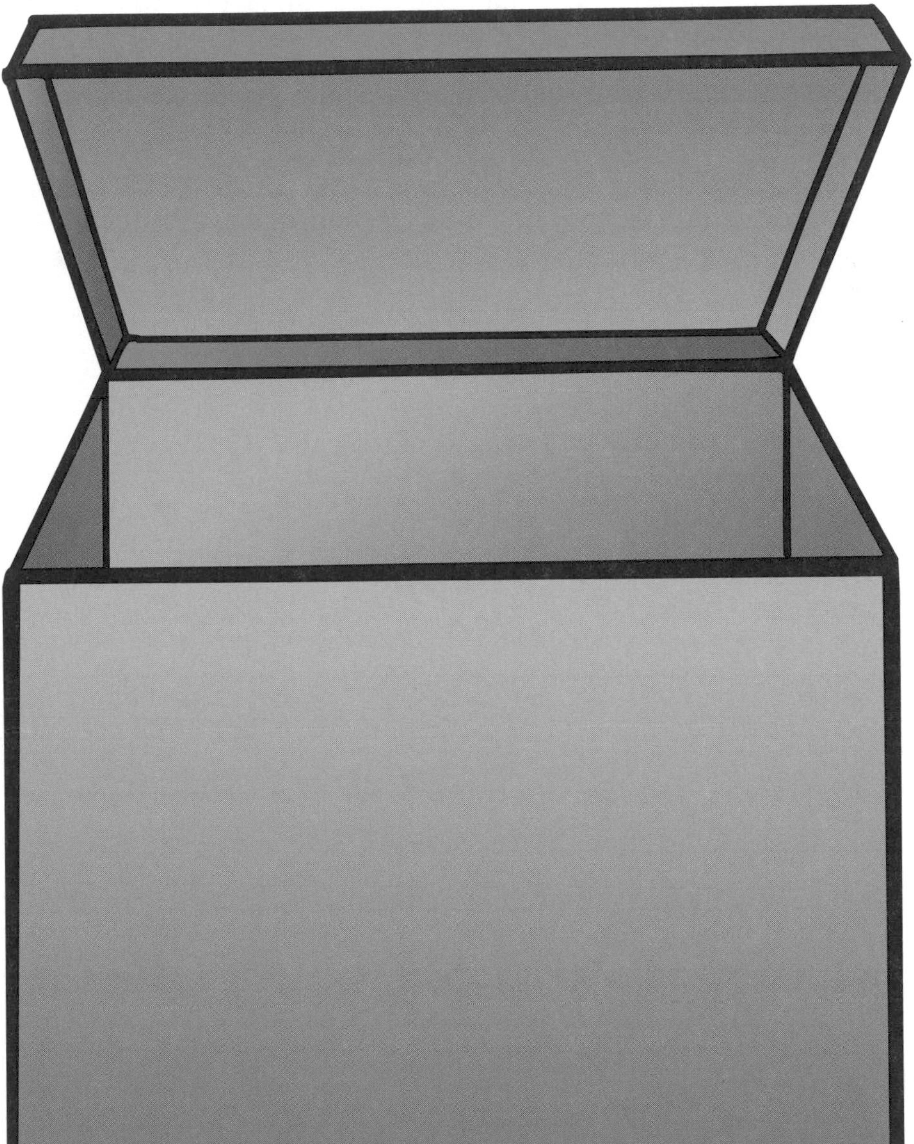

Jehovah

God's loving-kindness never goes away.

And surely I am with you always, to the very end of the age.

Matthew 28:20

Always the Same

Do you take your favorite blanket or stuffed animal to bed at night? A long car ride is cozy with a special blanket and pillow along.

Saving things you loved when you were younger is OK. Sadly, blanket colors fade. Stuffed rabbits and bears lose stuffing over the years. Their ears, eyes and noses are sure to fall off. Toys and keepsakes do not last forever.

Things are not eternal (lasting forever). Only God, Jehovah, is eternal. His promises never fade away. Jehovah's loving-kindness will never wear out. He is the same today as He was yesterday.

Your Turn

1. Can you name someone or something that never changes?
2. Try to think of someone or something that never grows old or wears out.
3. Name a toy or keepsake you plan to have forever.

Prayer

I am so glad You never change, God. I am thankful You never wear out or get tired of me. Amen.

Teddy Bear Puzzle

The teddy bear is falling apart! Put the teddy bear back together by drawing in what is missing. The answers are on page 232.

God Is There

I can bow down to a holy God.

God said, "Take off your sandals, for the place where you are standing is holy ground."

Exodus 3:5

Moses, Moses!

An angel appeared to Moses in flames of fire from a bush. Moses saw the bush was on fire. But there was something strange about the fire. It was not burning up the bush.

"I must go closer to this strange bush. How can a bush burn and not burn up?" he thought.

God saw Moses walking toward the bush. So He called out to him, "Moses, Moses!"

"Here I am," said Moses.

"Don't come any closer but take off your sandals. The place where you stand is holy ground. I am the God of your parents," replied the Lord.

Moses removed his shoes and covered his face. He was afraid to look at God, even though God loved Moses. God is holy. Moses knew he could not look right at Him. Since God was at that place, the ground was made holy.

God told Moses at the burning bush, "I am who I am." God meant that He is a holy God who never changes.

Your Turn

1. Why did God ask Moses to take off his shoes?
2. What does taking your shoes off tell God?

Prayer

You are a holy God and I love You. I bow down to You and You alone. Amen.

The Burning Bush

Make a picture of what you think the burning bush looked like. Pray with your family. Take off your shoes and kneel to Jehovah (God), like Moses did at the burning bush.

God Is There

God is always with me.
So do not fear, for I am with you.
Isaiah 41:10

Favorite Firsts

Remember the first time you skated, rode a bike or played checkers? Those were favorite firsts.

Who was there when you had a favorite first? Maybe your sister was there for your first backbend. Your dad may have been there to take the training wheels off your bike. Was your grandpa there on your first hike up the hill? Was anyone else there?

There are also fearful firsts: the first time you were afraid to swim, the first time you jumped off a diving board or the first test at school. Maybe it was a relay in gym class.

God was, and is, there at every favorite and fearful first. God was there when the first baby bird fell from its nest. Surely He sees everything that happens to you. He has always been there for your favorite firsts.

Your Turn

1. How can God help you when you are afraid?
2. Why does God want to be at your favorite and fearful firsts?
3. Name a place where you want God to be with you.

Prayer

Thank You for caring for me, God. I am so glad You are always with me. Amen.

Favorite First Photos

Draw some of your favorite and fearful firsts to remind you that God is there.

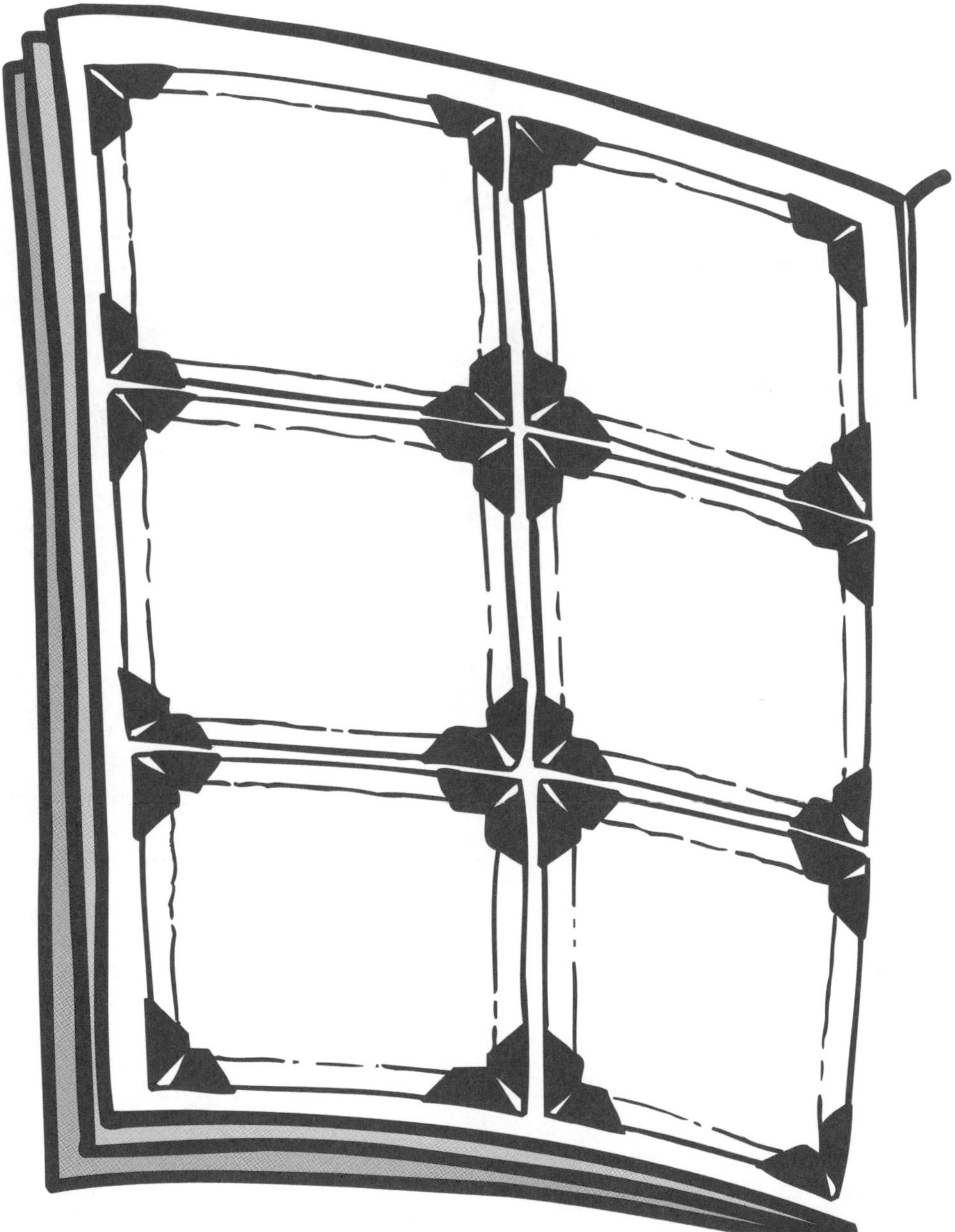

God Is There

God likes being with me.

Be still, and know that I am God.

Psalm 46:10

Quiet Places

"Be quiet! Shh! Stop talking. I can't hear the TV."

"I am trying to sleep, so leave me alone."

"Turn the radio down. It's killing my ears."

Noise is everywhere! Do you have a quiet place of your own? Under your bed? In the closet? What about the tree house? Maybe you have to get into the dog house! Is there anywhere you can go and not hear noise?

Jesus looked for quiet places. He got away from noise and crowds. One time He found a secret place. The place wasn't a tree house. The place wasn't a closet. It wasn't even a bedroom. This place was a garden.

The garden was one mile outside the walls around Jerusalem. He went there to pray and be alone with God. Jesus knew God wanted to talk with Him alone. God is there with you when it is noisy. He's there in the noise of TV. He's there in the noise of the radio. He likes being with you at quiet times, too. It's easier for God to speak to you in a quiet place.

Your Turn

1. Do you have quiet places at your house? Where?
2. Plan a time, with your parents' permission, when you can meet with God in one of these places.
3. Sit in a quiet place and tell God you like to be alone with Him.

Prayer

Show me quiet places where I can meet with You each day. Amen.

Quiet and Loud Places

Pretend the house below is your house. Think of inside and outside quiet places at your house. Can you talk to God there? Draw a Bible in each place in the house picture below where you can meet quietly with God to pray.

God Is There

God hears me when I call to Him.

You will seek me and find me when you seek me with all your heart.

Jeremiah 29:13

Looking for Something?

"I know I put it right here!"

"It couldn't have walked away. Grandma gave me that hair bow."

"That is my favorite doll. I'm not stopping until I find it." Seeking after God is not like looking for a missing hair bow or doll. God is not a thing, He is real. When you look for God you will find Him.

Can you call out to your bow or baby doll? A lost shoe may not be found for months but God promises He is there when you look for Him.

The Bible says in Jeremiah that when you look for God with all your heart, you will find Him. Call to Him and He will hear you.

Your Turn

1. How can you know God is real?
2. How do you look for God?
3. How can you show others God is real?

Prayer

Thank You, God, that I can call to You and You answer me. I want to seek You with all my heart. Please show me You are there, Lord. Amen.

My Journal Page

Use the area below as a journal page to write to God. Tell Him about friends and family. Share your deepest feelings.

God Is There

God is always watching over me.
The Lord will watch over your coming and going.
Psalm 121:8

Fire Trucks and Police Cars

Kathy lay in bed tossing and turning. She fluffed her pillow at least five times in one minute. As she lay under the canopy over her bed, she could hear sirens.

She wondered, "Are those sirens from fire trucks or police cars? Maybe they are both."

Her mind kept imagining where they might be headed in the middle of the night.

"I am just thankful they are out there." She yawned.

Fire trucks and police cars move around your city at night. Friendly policemen and firemen are there for you. Police cars patrol neighborhoods and streets. They are always there. Firemen are at their stations waiting to be called to a fire. They are always there. Even though you can't see them because you are asleep, they are still there to protect you and help you.

That is the way God is. He is always there watching over you. You may be asleep, but God is there. No matter what time it is, God is there. No matter where you go, God is there.

Your Turn

1. What are some ways God protects you?
2. How do you feel, knowing God is watching over you?
3. God will never stop watching over you. How can you show Him that you like His watchful care?

Prayer

Thank You, God, for being there. I am so glad You love me and are there to watch over my days and nights. Amen.

The Phone

Color the phone. Learn that 911 is the phone number you should call in case of an emergency. Read Psalm 23. Find the verse in Psalm 23 that tells you not to fear, for God is with you. Write it on the receiver of the phone to remind you that God is there.

God the Shepherd

God is my shepherd.

The Lord is my shepherd, I shall not be in want.

Psalm 23:1

The Shepherd's Sheep, Part One

"It's time to turn the lights out. Go to sleep, Ruthie," Mother said.

"I can't go to sleep, Mom!" Ruthie replied. "I'm worried about my speech contest at school tomorrow."

"I'd feel nervous, too, Ruthie. But don't worry; you're ready for it. Besides, God the Shepherd will be at the contest."

"The Shepherd? I thought shepherds just took care of sheep!"

"That is right, Ruthie." Mother rubbed her back. "God is like a shepherd. He cares for you. He wants to help you in everything you do. You are like a little lamb to Him when you let Him care for your needs."

"Tell me more about the Shepherd and His sheep, Mom," Ruthie yawned.

"We'll talk about sheep some more tomorrow night. Right now you need to get to sleep."

"OK! Good night."

Your Turn

1. What are you worried about?
2. Are you one of God's little sheep?
3. How can you make it easy for God the Shepherd to care for you?

Prayer

I want to be Your lamb, God. Teach me to stay close to You, my Shepherd. Amen.

Shepherd Maze

Help the lamb get to the shepherd, then color the maze pictures. Draw a line to the safety of the shepherd.

God the Shepherd

God will help me when I am afraid.

The Lord is my shepherd, I shall not be in want.

Psalm 23:1

The Shepherd's Sheep, Part Two

"Sheep with a loving shepherd don't worry about what will happen to them," Mother told Ruthie.

"Do you know that sheep are easily scared?" Mother asked. "They don't sleep well if they're hungry. They don't sleep well when pesky flies crowd around, either. Sheep can't rest when the other sheep tease them in their pen. A good shepherd makes sure his flock is safe from wild animals. He makes sure his sheep have lots of green grass to eat. A shepherd rubs oil on the noses of his sheep to help keep flies and gnats away."

"It makes my nose itch just hearing about it!" said Ruthie. "Can God be my Shepherd?"

"Yes, God is your good Shepherd!" Mother replied. "He will help you with fear and worry. Let's pray to your good Shepherd right now and ask Him for help." Mother held Ruthie's hand as they prayed together.

Your Turn

1. What do you worry about?
2. Does God help you not to worry?
3. What can a sheep do to stay safe and out of trouble?
4. What can you do to stay out of trouble?

____

____

____

____

____

____

____

____

Prayer

God, I am worried about ______________. Will You help me? Thank You for being my Shepherd. Amen.

Sheep's Pen Chart

Read Psalm 23. List three things you learned about God as a shepherd in Psalm 23.

____

____

____

God the Shepherd

I can listen and obey when God speaks.

My sheep listen to my voice; I know them, and they follow me.

John 10:27

Voices

"Hello, Kate?"

"No, this is Julie."

"I'm sorry, Julie. I didn't recognize your voice. You sound like your older sister on the phone."

Voices are like snowflakes and fingerprints. No two are alike. Sometimes you can know a person by hearing his or her voice.

Voices can be loud. Voices can be quiet. Voices can be hard or soft. What kind of voice do you have?

God also has a voice! But you may not hear it out loud. You can hear God by reading the Bible. The Bible tells you God's words. God also speaks to you in your heart and mind, like when you are sad for someone who is treated badly. That sad feeling may be God telling you to help that person.

The Bible says "The Lord is my shepherd" in Psalms 23:1. In this verse God's voice is telling you He loves you. It also tells you He wants to care for you.

Have you ever thought about hitting your brother or sister? Choosing not to hit may have been God talking to you. God speaks! Do you listen and obey?

Your Turn

1. Can you think of any times when God spoke to you?
2. Where do you think God is when He speaks to you?
3. Where are you when you listen for God?

Prayer

God, I know You love me and want to speak to me. I will be a good listener when You speak to me. Amen.

God Speaks

Make a tape recording of your voice and listen to it. Did you know your voice sounds that way? Draw a picture in each square below of when God has spoken to you in your mind, in your heart and in the Bible. If you did not listen and obey, ask Him to help you next time. Write down that you did or did not listen and obey.

God spoke to me in my mind.

____

____

God spoke to me in my heart.

____

____

When God speaks, I should listen.

God spoke to me in the Bible.

____

____

God the Shepherd

God knows me.

I am the good shepherd; I know my sheep and my sheep know me.

John 10:14

My Sheep Know Me

Christy Franks lives on my side of the street. She lives at the end of our block. Her house is the only red house for miles. Christy is my age, 8 years old. We aren't in the same class at school.

Christy has a 12-year-old brother and 3-year-old sister. Her dad drives an old blue car to work each day. Her mother stays home with Christy's little sister, Amy.

Christy has short, reddish hair and freckles. She wears jeans and a sweatshirt to school.

Does this sound as if I am describing someone I know well? I don't even know Christy Franks! She doesn't know me. I know about her because I see her in the school lunchroom. I see her playing in front of her house. My mother tells me about her family. I know facts about Christy Franks, but I don't really know her. I don't know if she likes ice cream or hamburgers. I don't know if Christy is caring or helpful.

Is there someone you only know about but don't know well? What about God? God is like a shepherd who knows his sheep. You are like one of His sheep. Are you a sheep who knows your Shepherd?

Your Turn

1. What do you know about God?
2. How can you get to know God?
3. How do you act toward someone you know? How do you act toward God?

Prayer

I want to know You, God. Show me Yourself. Amen.

Whom Do I Know?

Draw a picture of yourself inside the heart. Just as a shepherd loves his sheep, God loves you! Make a list in the box of children you know but don't know well. Call someone from your list. Invite them to your house after school or on Saturday. Play a game called Ten Questions. Take turns asking each other questions, like what is your favorite food or game.

The God Who Satisfies

God satisfies my heart.
He satisfies (fills) the thirsty.
Psalm 107:9

God Fills My Heart

"Grandma, you make the best fried chicken in the whole world!" Kelly cried, as she sat staring at her fourth drumstick.

"I don't think I can eat another bite," she groaned.

She dragged her fork through the center of her potato pond. "I have had enough, my stomach is telling me it is happy now."

"Kelly, I am glad I could give your stomach what it needs," replied Grandmother with a smile.

What does it take to fill you up? What makes you happy? Is it a new doll, or a bracelet and necklace? Is it many friends? Maybe it's a good-night kiss from your mom or dad.

Grandma satisfied the needs of Kelly's stomach. God can satisfy the needs of your heart. Water satisfies your thirst. God satisfies your heart. Will you let Him satisfy you?

Your Turn

1. What are some needs of your heart?
2. How can God make you feel satisfied?
3. What does it mean to be hungry for God?

Prayer

Dear God, I give You the needs of my heart. Please show me You love me so I won't want as many toys and things. Amen.

Satisfaction Jugs

In Jug A, draw toys you think you need to satisfy you and make you happy. Draw a heart in Jug B to show that God can satisfy your heart needs.

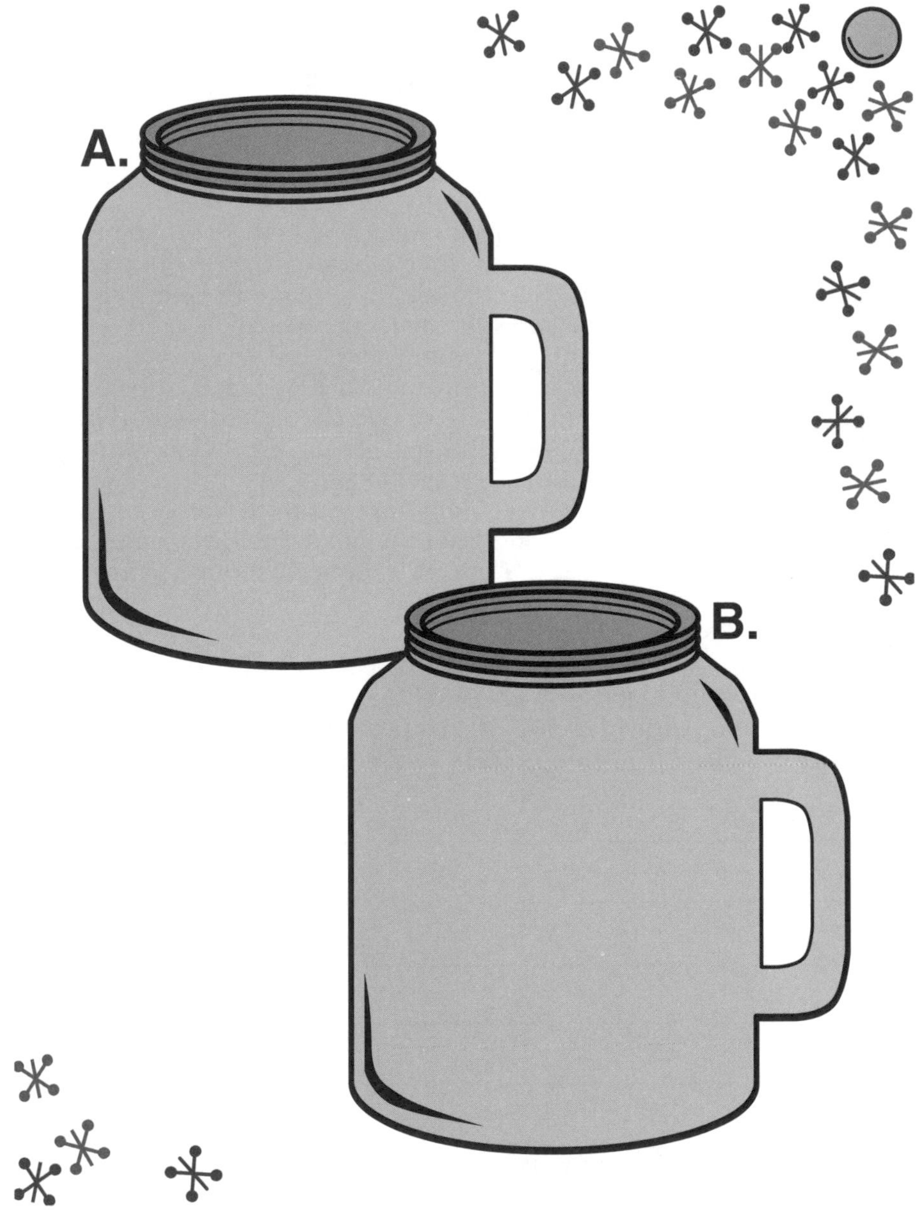

The God Who Satisfies

I will follow God's recipe for me.

You...satisfy the desires of every living thing.

Psalm 145:16

God's Recipe

"Stop! That is enough flour, Sally," said Mom as she dried her hands on the kitchen towel. "One cup will be enough for this apple cake recipe."

Sally smiled. "What would happen if we didn't put enough flour in the recipe, Mom?"

"Well, It wouldn't taste right, Sal. I'm afraid we would end up with a runny cake," replied Mom.

"Wouldn't just a little more flour and butter be better?" asked Sally.

"No," replied Mom. "One cup of flour is enough. More butter won't help either. There is just enough in the recipe to make the cake come out perfect. If we follow the recipe, we will have a tasty cake."

Mom thought for a moment. "You know, Sal, God has a recipe for our lives, too. He gives just the right measure of what we need to be satisfied and happy. We must follow Him closely to find the ingredients in life. His recipe for us is to be satisfied as we live our life for Him. God wants us to tell our friends and family about His recipe for life."

Mom put the cake into the oven. Sally jumped from her stool. "I want to follow God's recipe for me. I don't want my life to be like a runny cake," said Sally. "Great! Now let's set the table for dinner," replied Mom.

Your Turn

1. Where can you find God's recipe for life?
2. What are some things He puts in recipes for His people to help them be satisfied? (Example: love, peace, etc.)

____

____

____

____

____

Prayer

Thank You, God, for giving me just enough love to make me satisfied with all I have. Thank You for having a recipe for my life so I can know You and be satisfied. Amen.

My Measuring Cup

Is your measuring cup full? Are you satisfied? List four things next to the cup that satisfy you. Is God on your list? Do you think everything on the list is part of God's recipe for your life? Color the cup to the full line.

1. ______________________

2. ______________________

3. ______________________

4. ______________________

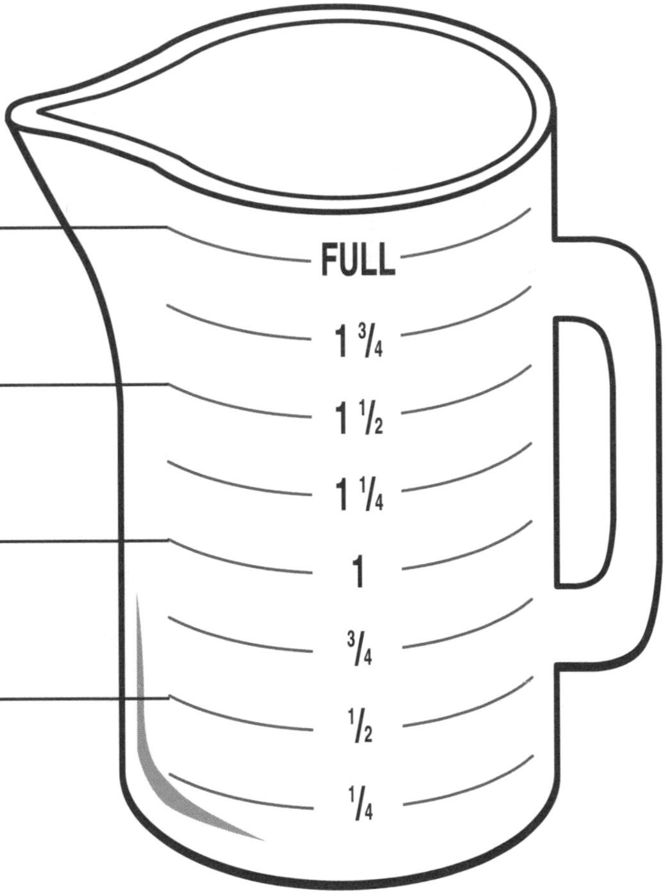

God, My Father

God is a happy father when I am well.

Give thanks to the Lord, for he is good;
his love endures forever.

Psalm 106:1

A Happy Father

Have you ever been sick and stayed home from school? Have you been in the hospital? Your parents worry about you when you are sick.

The Bible tells of a little girl who was so sick that she died. Her father, Jairus, was an important man in the city. He bowed before Jesus and said, "My little girl has been very sick. Please make her well again."

Jesus loved the little girl and her father. He stopped what He was doing. He went with the father to their house. Friends came outside to greet them. They said, "Your little girl is dead."

Jairus put his face in his hands and cried. Jairus was a loving father like God, our heavenly Father. Jesus said to Jairus, "Don't be afraid. Believe in Me and the Father in heaven will heal your child."

The girl's family was sobbing for her. "The girl is only asleep," said Jesus. He took the girl's hand and said, "My child, get up." At once she stood up!

Her father was happy and surprised. He hugged and kissed his little girl. Now he was a happy father. What a wonderful Father we have in heaven!

Your Turn

1. Do you think God was a happy Father when the girl was healed? Why?
2. How does the Father in heaven feel when you are sick or have a problem?
3. Can you ask your earthly father to pray for you when you are sick?

____

____

____

____

____

Prayer

Thank You, God, for caring for me and loving me like a father should. Thank You for caring for me like my father does. Amen.

My Father's Footprints

Color the footprints from your house all the way to God's house in heaven.

God, My Father

God is my loving heavenly father.
Abba, Father,...everything is possible for you.
Mark 14:36

Abba Father

When you tie two ropes together they become one rope. When you tie your shoe strings you bring the string around and tie it in a loop. You pull the strings tight together. The strings hold together.

When we say people are tied to each other we mean they are close together in love and friendship. In Bible days, the children called their own fathers "Abba." The word meant closeness, love and respect. It showed that a child had a special tie with her father.

The people who lived in the days when Jesus was on earth called God "Abba Father." The words showed close family feelings between God and people. People who knew God well, thought of Him as a father. They saw that He cared for them. He loves you, too, with the best father-like love, no matter what you do. He takes care of you when you are sick. He listens to the hurts in your heart.

Your Turn

1. How can you let God be your "Abba Father"?
2. Why does God want you to call Him "Abba Father"?
3. How can you show respect for your earthly father?

Prayer

Abba Father, my God, I love You. I want You to be my heavenly Father. I want to be close to You each day. Amen.

Father's Bow

Write Abba Father and your name (or draw yourself) in the center of the giant bow. Color the bow to remind you that Abba Father is a special name for your heavenly Father. Remember that God wants to be tied to you like a bow.

Where Is God?

God has a happy family with Him in heaven.
In my Father's house are many rooms.
John 14:2

Heaven, God's Home

What does your house look like inside? Is there a family room? How many bedrooms and bathrooms are in your house? What color is the wallpaper and furniture?

Did you know the Bible tells us where God lives? His house is in a place called heaven. Heaven is the place where God and Jesus live. But God and Jesus are not alone in their house, just as you are not alone in your house. God has a big family with Him in heaven. He is circled by angels who serve Him.

People who love and follow Jesus are promised a place in heaven. When a new baby is born, the family prepares a special room for that child. The room is the nursery. It holds things needed to love and care for the baby. Jesus left this earth to go prepare a special place for people He loves and who love Him. His room is a place where all believers and angels join in unending worship to God. It is a home where there is great happiness. Everyone in heaven shares in God's work.

Your Turn

1. How far away is heaven?
2. Why would God make a place for you in heaven?
3. What do you think God's work in heaven would be?

Prayer

Thank You, Jesus, for preparing a special place for me in heaven. Thank You, God, for loving me and inviting me to Your house someday. Amen.

God's Home

Make a picture at the bottom of the page showing what you think your place in heaven will look like.

Where Is God?

Praises to God are day and night in heaven.
Lord, God Most High, Creator of heaven and earth.
Genesis 14:22

Heaven Is a Treasure

Heaven is not a treasure chest, but it is a treasure house. A treasure is something of great value or worth. Heaven is a house of great worth because it is where God and Jesus live.

There are no churches or temples in heaven because God and Jesus are temples. In God's treasure house there is no pain, crying or weakness. You will never get tired or sleepy in heaven. There is only peace, happiness and joy in God's heavenly house. There aren't even chores to do in heaven. God's house is always sparkling clean and bright. Everything looks like a jewel.

The angels sing many praises to God and Jesus there: "Holy, Holy, Holy, only You are Holy God." Praises to God and Jesus go on day and night and forever in heaven. Praising God makes us happy and it pleases God.

In heaven everyone will praise God. You will be happy forever. Praise to God is better than gold and silver.

Your Turn

1. How can God be a temple? (A temple is a place of prayer and worship, like a church.)
2. Why do praises go on day and night in heaven?
3. Why is there peace, happiness and joy in heaven, but not on earth?

____

____

____

____

____

____

Prayer

Thank You, God, for heaven. I want to praise You and thank You for being God and loving me. Amen.

Treasure Chest Drawing

Draw pictures or write the names for some of the treasures in heaven mentioned in the devotion at left.

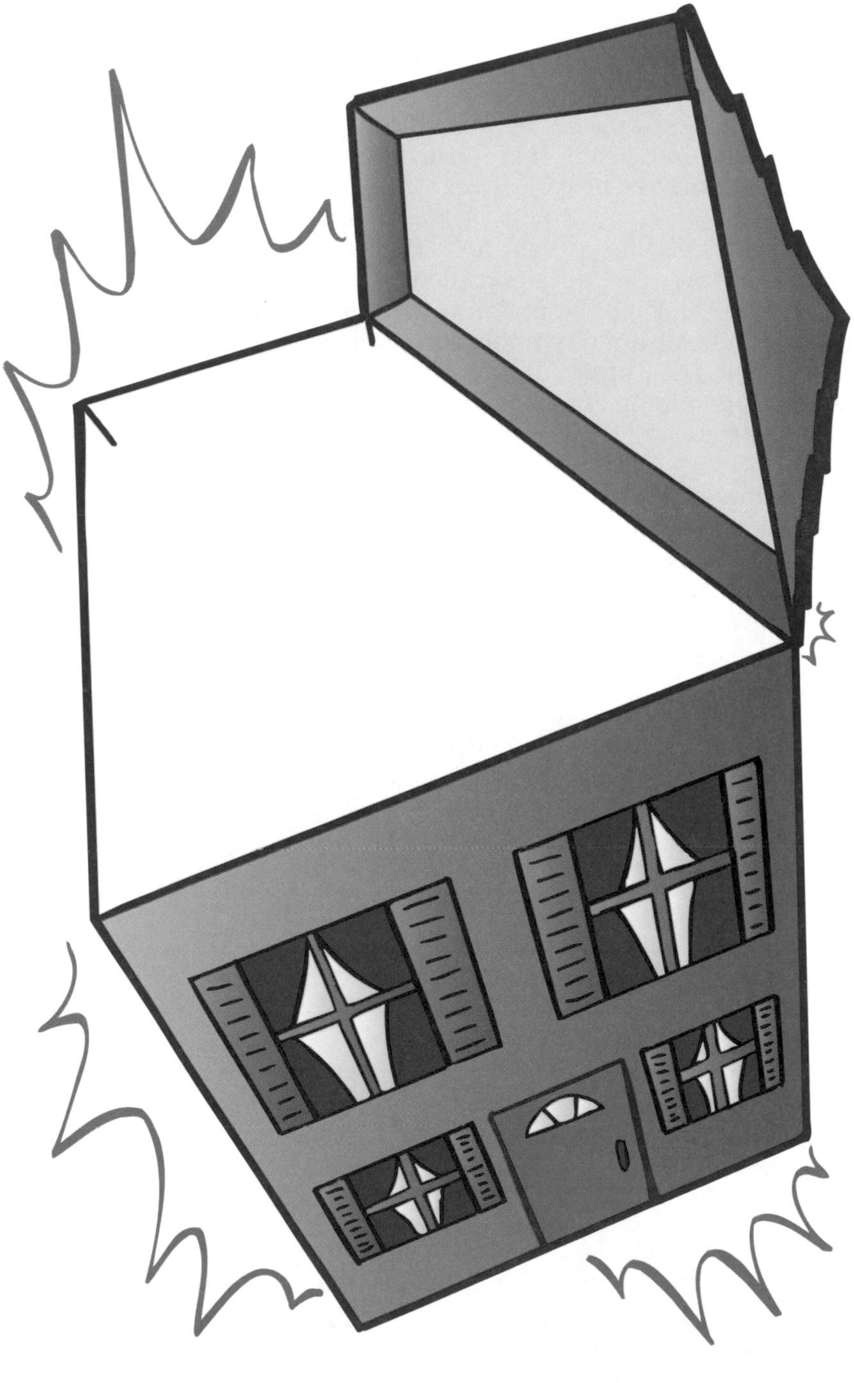

Where Is God?

Heaven is a beautiful place.
The great street of the city was of pure gold.
Revelation 21:21

Streets of Gold

John, one of God's disciples, was able to see heaven. He wrote down everything he saw in heaven. He reported heaven as a beautiful place. The colors shone brightly in heaven. Every color of the rainbow was at God's throne.

John saw no need for a night light there. God and Jesus are heaven's lights, so there is no sun and moon there. Doors and gates opened up to a beautiful throne. Angels surrounded God's throne with songs of praise.

There was a beautiful city in heaven with streets of gold. An angel also showed John the river of life. It flowed from the throne of God and Jesus. It went down the middle of the great street of the city. On each side of the river grew the trees of life. The trees carried twelve kinds of fruit on their branches.

The servants of the Lord in heaven were able to see God face-to-face. God's name was written on their foreheads.

Can you tell others how beautiful heaven will be? If you have ever wondered about heaven, you don't need to. Read about it in God's Word, in Revelation 22.

Your Turn

1. Why do you think God showed His home to John?
2. Why do you think God and Jesus light up heaven?
3. Would you like to be with God in heaven some day?

____

____

____

____

____

____

Prayer

Thank You, God, for telling John about Your home. I am glad to know where You live. I like Your house, God. Amen.

Streets of Gold

Find your way through the streets of gold to the throne of God and Jesus. Write the Scripture from the page at left at the bottom of this page. Draw your face on the girl below. Write God's name on your forehead.

God Loves Me

God wants to be my friend.
He was called God's friend.
James 2:23

Special Friend

Have you ever had to move to a new neighborhood and go to a new school? You wanted a new special friend. A special friend is someone who likes being with you.

A friend spends time with you on the playground. You go to birthday parties together. Special friends trade hair bows and doll clothes. Friends share friendship bracelets. They know when you have a bad day and they can cheer you. A special friend listens to you.

With a special friend, you can be yourself, even if it means being silly, sad, quiet or loud. Your friend is always there.

Special friends your age are nice to have, but God is the best friend to have. Abraham was God's friend. You can be one of His friends, too. He wants to hear from you each day. Your secrets are important to God. God loves at all times and in every way. He would like to be your special friend. Will you let Him be your best friend?

Your Turn

1. Do you have a special friend? What is your special friend like?
2. What does it mean to be a friend?
3. How can you be a good friend to God?

Prayer

Thank You for being my friend. Teach me to be a good friend, too. Amen.

God and Me!

Decorate and color the friendship necklace. Write "God and Me" on the necklace to remind you that God is your friend.

God Loves Me

God's love for me is great.
So great is his love.
Psalm 103:11

I Love You!

"Daddy, when will you be back from your trip?" asked Dana.

"In about three days," he said as he closed his briefcase.

"Oh. Do you have to go? I will really miss you, Daddy."

"I'll be back before you know it, Peanut. Besides, Grandma will take good care of you. Don't forget, I love you."

"I love you too, Daddy."

What makes you feel loved? Has anyone told you, "I love you"? Did it make you feel happy? Did it make you feel secure and safe? Those words probably make you feel so good that you want to go higher and higher on your backyard swing.

"I love you" is nice to hear over and over again. How many ways does God say "I love you?" How often does He say those words in the Bible? Many times! He wants us to be close to Him.

Like Dana's father, God loves you no matter what He is doing. God's love is stronger than the strongest man on earth. It's deeper than the deepest well in the ground. God's love is taller than the highest mountain peak. His love is like a gift for you to take right now. God is saying to you, "I love you!" Will you take God's great love for yourself? Go and tell others of His love.

Your Turn

1. Why does God love you?
2. Have you told someone you love him or her? Have you told members of your family?

Prayer

God, I take Your love into my heart and life. Thank You for loving me. Amen.

I Love You, God

Tell God you love Him using the five fingers of love. Trace your hand on the page and write each of the words below on a finger. Do all five fingers of love each time you pray. Count through them now.

Thanks: Thank You for Your love to me.
Sing: You are a God worth loving.
Obey: I will read and obey the Bible because I love You.
Tell: I love You, God.
Pray: I pray that my friends will know Your love.

God Loves Me

God chooses me.

You did not choose me, but I chose you.

John 15:16

Chosen One

Have you ever been the last one to be picked for team games at school? Have you ever raised your hand in the school classroom, but not been called on? Do you come from a loud family where you can't get a word in?

There is someone who chooses you every time and will never leave you out. There is someone who will let you get a word in. It is God! He wants to hear you. He wants to listen to your heart feelings every time.

Matthew 10:29 says "Not one [sparrow] will fall to the ground apart from the will of your Father." He doesn't leave out the sparrow, so surely He wouldn't leave you out. Just as God chose each star in the sky, God chose you. If God chose you, He willingly picked you. He wanted you and took you as someone He wants to be close to. God has chosen you to know Him.

Your Turn

1. If God picks you to belong to Him, what should you do?
2. How can you know God more?
3. How should you treat others who aren't chosen for games at school?

____

____

____

____

____

____

____

____

Prayer

Thank You, God, for choosing me and making me feel special to You. I don't know why You would choose me, but I am glad You did. Amen.

Choose Me

Look up the following words in a dictionary: select, pick, favor, choose and prefer. Write these words below on the blank lines.

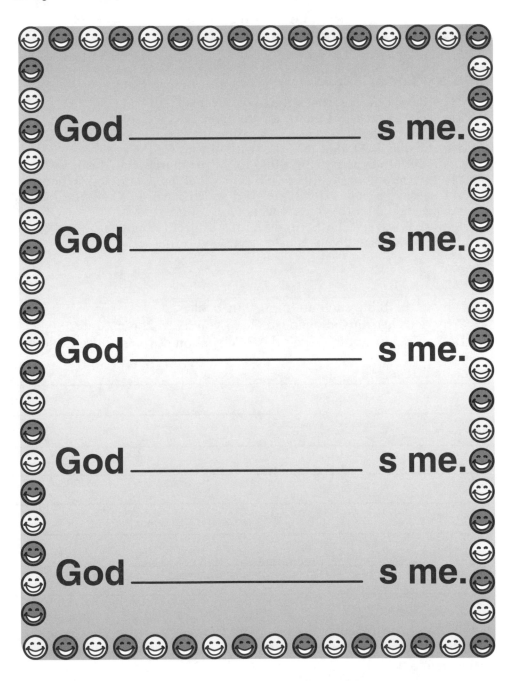

God __________________ s me.

God __________________ s me.

God __________________ s me.

God __________________ s me.

God __________________ s me.

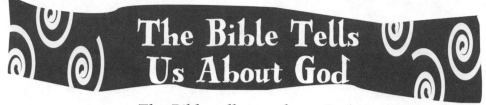

The Bible Tells Us About God

The Bible tells me about God.

The Word became flesh (a man) and made his dwelling among us.

John 1:14

God's Word, Jesus

"The B-I-B-L-E. Yes, that's the book for me."

"Jesus loves me this I know, for the Bible tells me so."

Songs and rhymes help you to learn that the Bible is God's Word. The Bible is the only book that tells the truth of who God is.

God sent Jesus as a living Bible to tell us about Him. Jesus is God's Son. He is like a living Word of God sent to tell us about God. When you listen to Jesus you are listening to God and His Word. When you look at what Jesus did on earth, you see what God is like.

John 5:39 says, "The Scriptures…testify [tell] about me." Stop, look and listen to Jesus and you will see what God is like.

Your Turn

1. Why is the Bible such an important book?
2. Why does learning about Jesus help you learn about God?
3. Do you read the Bible each day? Why should we read the Bible?

____

____

____

____

____

____

____

____

Prayer

Thank You, God, for Jesus, the living Word of God. Help me to read my Bible each day so I can know what God is like. Amen.

Bible Tracks

Use this page to track your Bible reading each day for two weeks. Color in the footprints each day you read your Bible. This will help you to remember to read each day. (You could copy the page to use over and over.) Be sure you have a Bible that you can read or your mom or dad can read to you. If you have never read the Bible before, start with the book of Mark. Ask for help with new words as you read, and write them below. Happy reading!

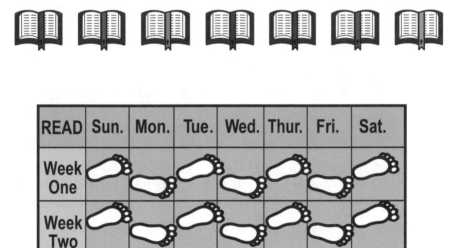

READ	Sun.	Mon.	Tue.	Wed.	Thur.	Fri.	Sat.
Week One							
Week Two							

New Words

____

____

____

____

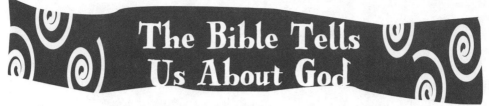

The Bible Tells Us About God

Reading the Bible is like eating honey.
How sweet are your words to my taste, sweeter than honey to my mouth!
Psalm 119:103

God's Words Are Sweet

"Someone is at the door!" yelled Mom.

"I'll get it," said Ann as she ran to the door.

"Hello," a small voice chimed. "Would you like to buy some honey to help children who can't walk?"

"Oh Mom, it's Honey Sunday for disabled children. This girl is selling honey in bear-shaped jars. Can we get one, Mom? Please! Honey tastes so sweet and good. Besides, I want to help others if I can."

"Sure," said Mom. "I've been hungry for a honey and peanut butter sandwich."

God's words in the Bible are like Ann's honey — they are sweet to the ears. His words are sweet when God tells of His love for the world. John 3:16 says "For God so loved the world that he gave his one and only Son" to die for us.

God's words are sweet because they say He can heal a broken body and heart. The Bible is sweet to people who don't know Jesus and His love for them. When they read it for the first time, it is like tasting honey. They want to read more and more because it tastes so good.

Ann helped children when she bought the sweet honey. When you read God's Word, you will learn of God's sweetness to you and others. God's word is sweet. It can make you sweet like honey. Tell others about the sweetness of God's word.

Your Turn

1. Why does God's Word seem sweet to people?
2. Why do people read and love the Bible?
3. Do you know a Bible verse or story that is sweet to you?

Prayer

Thank You, God, for Your sweet messages that tell me You love me. You want me to be Your child. The promises in Your Word are sweet like honey. Amen.

My Bible Search

Look at the jar of honey. Fill it with sweet words from the Bible. You can put favorite verses from this book in the jar. Fill it each day with a new or old verse as you learn God's sweetness.

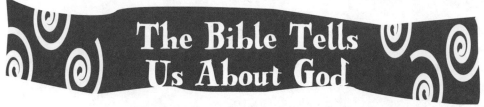

The Bible Tells Us About God

God is the greatest king of all.
You are my King and my God.
Psalm 44:4

What Makes a Good King?

Let's play a thinking game! Say out loud what comes to your mind when you see each of these words: bow, crown, rule, master, leader, Lord.

If you thought of a king after each word, you are a good guesser! Kings and queens are important. The king is the leader of everything. There were many kings in the Bible. Kings have ruled over cities or nations for many years.

In Bible times, a king was chosen because his father was king. A king in the Bible was good if he helped the people follow God's ways. The people loved good kings. They did whatever they could to show them their love.

A not-so-good king was one who didn't love God and didn't help his kingdom love God. Today there are more kinds of leaders than just kings. Some leaders are called president or mayor. Some are called governor or senator. But today's leaders are also good if they love God and follow His ways.

The true King is the one you should follow. He is God, the King of everyone and everything.

Your Turn

1. What kind of king would you follow?
2. Who is your true king? Is there anything God is not king over?
3. How can you tell if a leader of today loves God?

Prayer

God, You are the King of all. Teach me to follow You as my King. Help all the leaders and kings of the earth to love You. You are my God and I will give You thanks. Amen.

God, My King

God should be King in every area of your life. Draw crowns on the heads below that show how you should live if God is your King.

God's Rules

God wants me to follow His rules.

Obey the Lord your God and carefully follow all his commands.

Deuteronomy 28:1

Why Rules?

Kate listened carefully on the first day of school as Mrs. Green gave the classroom rules.

Every year I hear the same rules, she thought.

"Rules are important," said Mrs. Green. "Do you know the rules of the road? Ride your bike on the right side of the street. Signal all bike turns with a raised hand. Table rules say you should keep one hand in your lap at all times while eating. Classroom rules say you raise your hand before talking. Remember to keep hands and feet to yourself. Swimming rules say don't dive in shallow water. Always walk, don't run by the pool side."

Mrs. Green spoke quietly. "Rules are put in our path for a reason. Most rules help us learn to be safe and keep others safe. Some are created to make life easier."

Kate knew Mrs. Green was right. Rules need to be in place.

God gave you some special rules, too. God's rules keep you safe and show you when you are doing wrong in God's eyes. Doing wrong in God's eyes is called sin. God's rules are called The Commandments. There are ten in all and they are listed in the Old Testament of the Bible in Exodus 20. Do you know them?

Your Turn

1. What are some rules you follow at home?
2. Why do your parents have rules for you?
3. Why would God want you to follow rules?

____

____

____

____

____

____

Prayer

Thank You, God, for loving me enough to give me rules. You must want to protect me from sin. You are a good God! Amen.

Rules to Follow

Make a list of four rules on the board below. Think of rules that your parents and God would like you to follow. Write your rules and try to follow them. Tell your parents your rules.

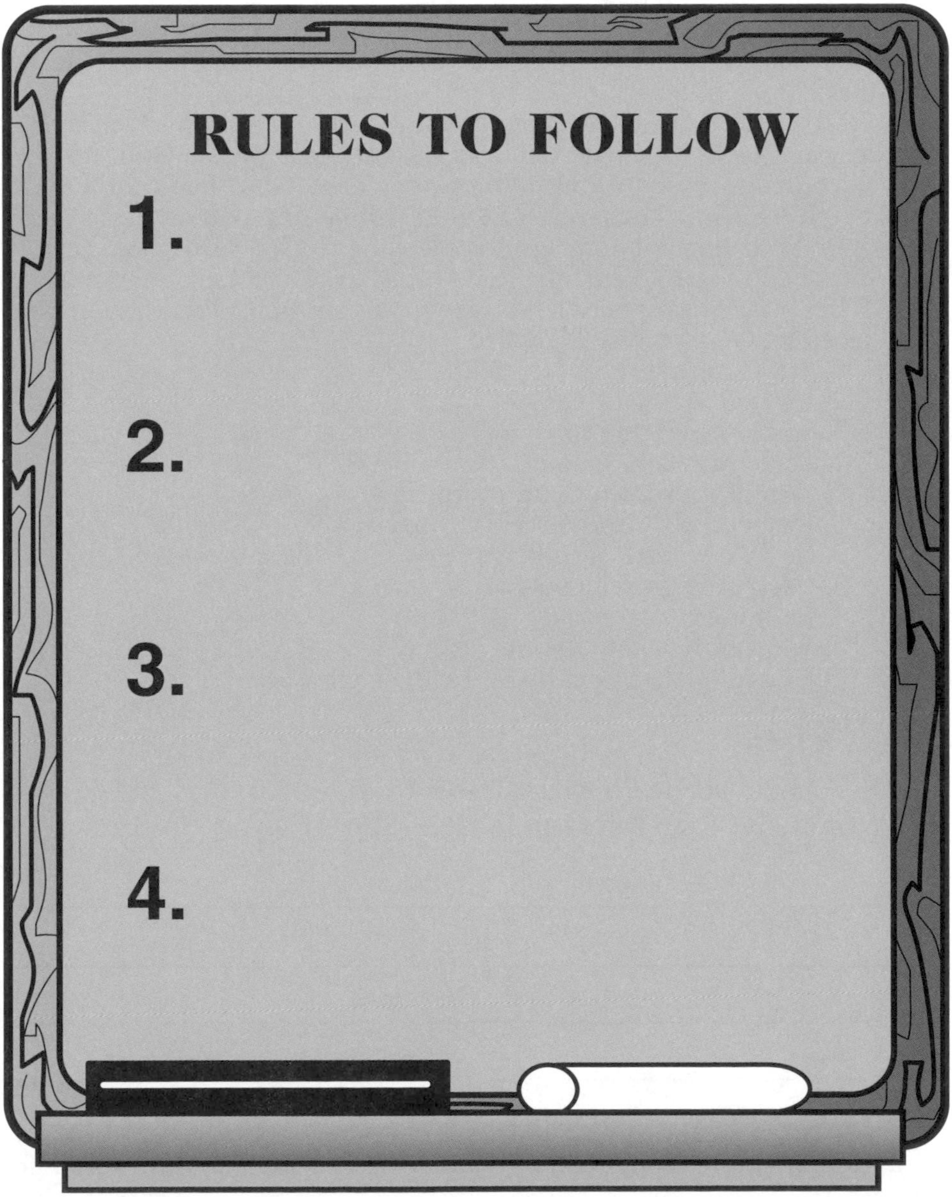

God's Rules

I like learning to please God.
Find out what pleases the Lord.
Ephesians 5:10

Pleasing God

"I hope she likes this card," said Cindy with a smile. Her class wanted to surprise their teacher with handmade birthday cards. Cindy really wanted to please Mrs. Carroll. She was the best teacher she had ever had.

"It's OK to want to please your teachers, Cindy," said Dad. "When you please your teachers and parents, you please God, too."

Your desire should always be to please God. Keep looking for ways to please Him. Then you and God will be happy together.

Do your hands know what is pleasing to God? Do your feet? Do your eyes and mouth? Learning new things in school isn't always easy.

Learning what pleases God isn't easy, either. One place to start is by learning God's rules. They are:

1. Put God first.
2. Love God most.
3. Honor God's name.
4. Make Sundays special.
5. Honor your father and mother.
6. Respect and protect life.
7. Be true when you marry.
8. Keep only what is yours.
9. Be honest.
10. Want only what is yours.

Obey and please God by following each one.

Your Turn

1. Why should you learn what pleases God?
2. What do these ten rules sound like? (Hint: They are in Exodus.)

____

____

____

____

Prayer

Dear God, help me to remember what pleases You. Make me glad and able to please You. Amen.

I'm Pleasing God

Color the girl below and think of some ways to please God with your hands, feet, heart, lips, eyes and ears. Write your ideas by the different body parts to help you remember.

God's Rules

God wants me to love Him most of all.
You shall have no other gods before me.
Exodus 20:3

Do Put God First

What is first in: A-B-C? How about 1-2-3? Ready-Set-Go?

The A in A-B-C, the 1 in 1-2-3 and the Ready in Ready-Set-Go are first. God is the A in A-B-C. God is the 1 in 1-2-3 and the Ready in Ready-Set-Go.

The Bible says that nothing should be more important to you than God. The more you know God, the easier it is to put Him first. Wanting your own way isn't putting God first. When things like fun, toys and TV are more important to you than God, He isn't your A, 1 or Ready.

A story in the Bible tells about a rich man who put his money before God and Jesus. His life was very sad. Read about this man in the New Testament of the Bible in Luke 18:18-29. God loves you and wants you to love Him first.

Your Turn

1. What kinds of things are most important to you?
2. How can you warn friends not to let anyone but God be first in their lives?
3. If God is first, where will you be in A-B-C, 1-2-3 and Ready-Set-Go?

Prayer

Help me to follow You, God. Don't let anything or anyone be more important to me than You. Amen.

God First Puzzle

God's first rule is to always put Him first. Nothing should be more important to you than God. Use the pictures below to find the words for the crossword puzzle. The words in the puzzle are things that you might wrongly put before God. The answers are on page 232.

God's Rules

Loving God first is best.

You shall not make for yourself an idol (statues to worship).

Exodus 20:4

Do Love God Most

"Amy," called Mrs. Zinn. "Please look up here. We need to get this math lesson done before lunch time."

Amy was a daydreamer and she liked to pretend. She spent lots of school hours looking out the window.

Amy wanted a pony, but God had not given her one. So she was thinking about how to turn Tucker, her golden retriever dog, into a pony. She thought she could use a blanket as a saddle and a leash for the reins.

Amy had always wanted a little pony like Daisy, the one her grandpa kept in his barnyard. But she knew that no matter how hard she tried, Tucker would never be a pony. Only God can make ponies.

In Bible days, people made a person or animal from stone or gold. They called these statues their gods. The people thought that these idols were real. They worshipped and prayed to them.

No one can make statues be God, just like no one can make dogs be ponies. Today many people still make their own gods. Whatever you love the most can wrongly become your god. Your pretend gods aren't made of stone or gold. They could be TV, jewelry, candy or friends. The one true God deserves to be the one you love most. Which god do you love?

Your Turn

1. How will God know you love Him best?

2. Look up the word "idol" in the dictionary. What does it mean?

____

____

____

____

____

____

Prayer

I am glad You are my God. Please forgive me for not always loving You more than anything else. Help me to put You first in everything. Amen.

Secret Messages

Decode the secret message about loving God first. Use the heart dial to help you decode it. The answers are on page 232.

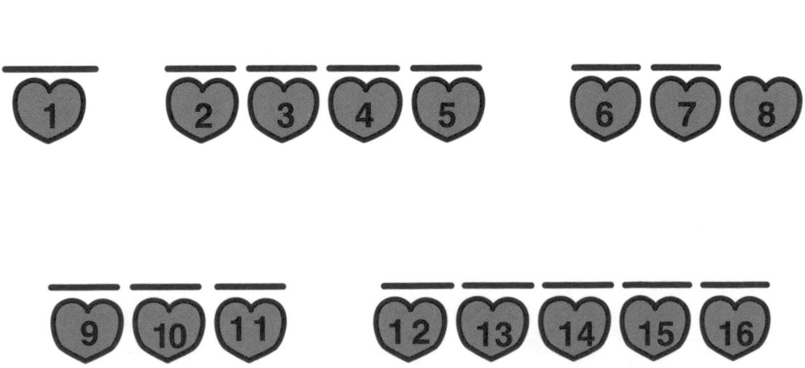

God's Rules

God loves for me to honor His name.

You shall not misuse the name of the Lord your God.

Exodus 20:7

Honor God's Name

Lazy-Lucy. Boy-Joy. Dopey-Hopey. Daffy-Kathy. Dianna-Banana.

These are all examples of names being misused. Has your name ever been turned into a bad or silly name? Sometimes people use a name when they have no reason. How do you feel when people use your name to tease you? Has anyone ever used your name wrongly when they were angry? How does that make you feel?

"Oh sweet Lucy, I love you!" How do you feel when your name is used in a loving way like that?

How should God's name be used? Some people use His name and Jesus' name in anger. Using any part of God's name wrongly, like when you lose a game, is sin. That makes God feel very sad. People use the name of God when they don't have a good reason to use it.

When and how should you use God's name? God loves His name to be used to tell others about Him and Jesus. He loves to hear His name mentioned when we are thankful. Always protect and honor His name.

Do you have enough boldness to defend His name? It will make Him happy if you always love and honor His name.

Your Turn

1. What are some wrong ways people use God's name?
2. How can you use the name of God in good ways?

Prayer

Dear God, I thank You for Your name. Your name is special to me and I love Your name. Show me how to use Your name in good ways. Amen.

God's Name Tags

Make three name tags for God. Write His name three different ways showing Him you love and honor His name. (Examples: Sweet Lord, King of Kings, Jehovah, etc.)

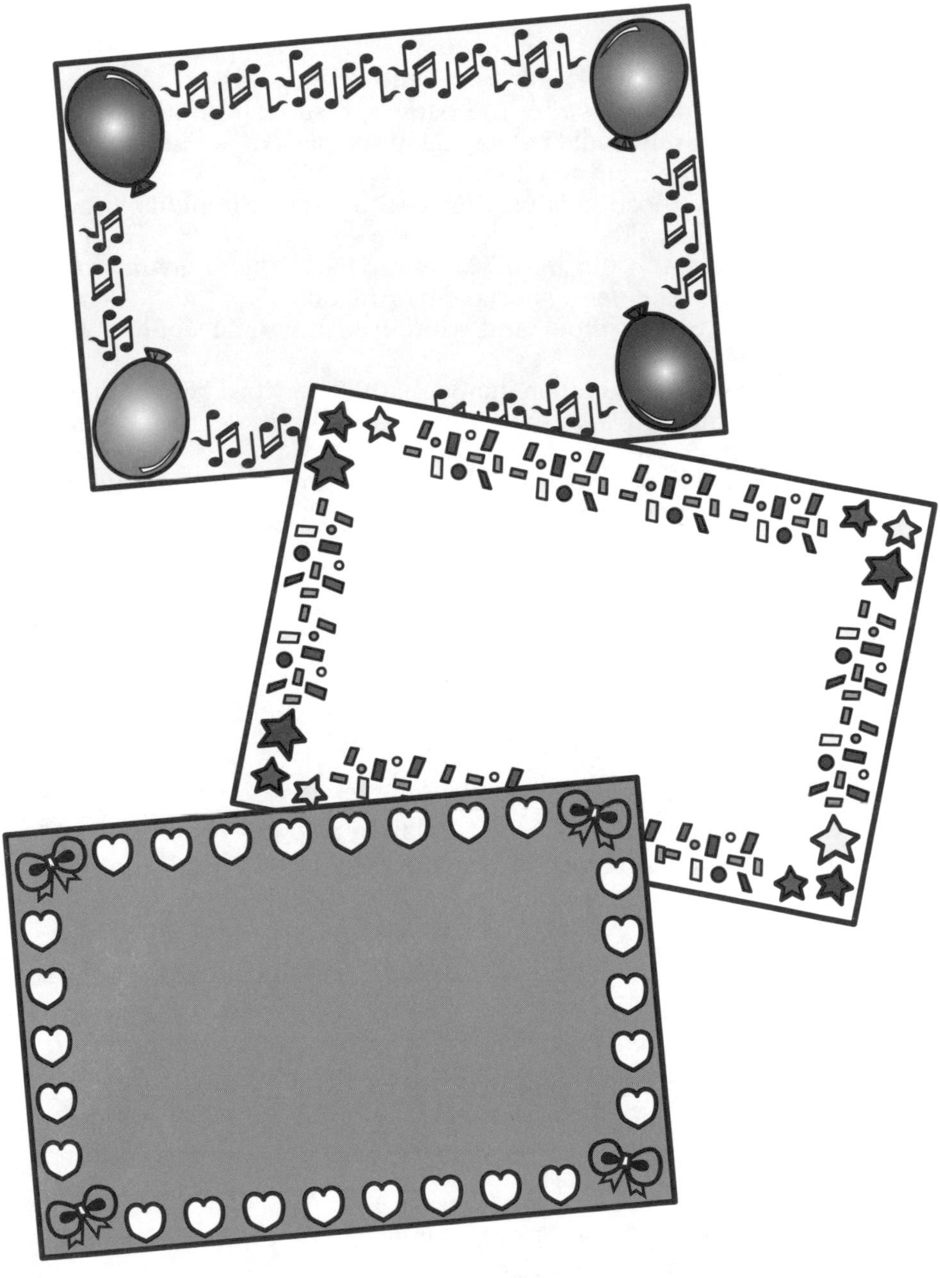

God's Rules

God makes Sunday a special day.

Remember the Sabbath day by keeping it holy.

Exodus 20:8

Make Sundays Special

As Sara's family drove home from church one Sunday, Sara noticed something. When they drove by the park, she saw children playing. She wondered why children would be playing in the park on a Sunday morning. She thought everyone went to church.

"Mom, why are those kids playing in the park? Shouldn't they be in Sunday school?" she asked.

"They may not know our Lord," Mom replied. "They may not know we should set Sundays aside as a special day for God."

Sara listened to her mom and wondered how she could tell those children about God.

The Bible says to remember the Sabbath. The word "Sabbath" comes from words that mean to rest from work. In Bible times, the Sabbath day was a day of worship — a gift to God.

Sunday is the day of worship and rest. You should also worship God at home each day through prayer and reading the Bible.

Another part of your worship to Him is doing good things for others, like telling the children Sara saw at the park about Jesus. God loves you and wants you to take care of yourself. You care for your mind and body when you rest from your everyday work and play on the Sabbath.

Your Turn

1. What do you do on Sundays?
2. Do you think it is OK with God to play in a sports event on Sunday?
3. What would you tell someone who says she knows Jesus, but doesn't go to church?

Prayer

God, help me to always keep Your day special. Teach me to use it to do something good for You. Amen.

Sunday Dolls

Matthew 12:9-13 tells that Jesus did good things for people on the Sabbath. Write on one doll what Jesus did that day, then write some of your own ideas of good things you can do on the Sabbath on the other dolls. When you are finished writing, color the dolls.

God's Rules

God is happy when I obey my parents.
Honor your father and your mother.
Exodus 20:12

Honor Your Father and Mother

"Jessie, you promised to empty the trash and pick up your toys. Grandmother tripped over one of your dolls. She could fall and get hurt," said Mom.

God's word says "honor your father and mother." That means that He wants you to listen, obey and love your parents. Parents need your honor and it pleases God when you love them. Honoring your parents is like promising to show them love and to obey them.

How can you honor your parents? Jessie had promised to pick up her toys. She didn't keep her promise. Her grandmother could have been hurt because she didn't honor her promise.

When you forget to honor our parents it hurts you and others. What can you do to keep from making the same mistake as Jessie?

Your Turn

1. Why does God want you to obey your parents?
2. Can you name a time when you obeyed your parents and you were glad you did?
3. Can you make a promise to God to obey your parents?

____

____

____

____

____

____

____

____

Prayer

Dear God, forgive me for the times when I haven't obeyed my parents. Help me to keep my promises and honor my parents. Amen.

The Promise Card

Can you promise God that you will try to honor your parents? Fill out the Promise Card below. Also, write a note to your parents on a different sheet of paper telling how you plan to honor and obey them.

I, ____________, pledge to honor
(your name)

my parents,

____________________ , my mother, and

____________________ , my father.

God's Rules

God gave me life as a gift.
You shall not murder.
Exodus 20:13

Respect and Protect Life

Each day the television news tells of people hurting other people. It is hard to watch and hear about people breaking God's rules. You shouldn't hurt anyone.

One of God's rules says "you shall not murder." Murder is killing a person. You may kill spiders and flies because they bother you. You might kill fish and chickens for food. God doesn't mean that kind of "kill" in this rule. He means murder or taking the life of a person.

God wants you to know how important every person is to Him. Your life, your parents, friends and babies not even born yet are all important to Him. The lives of older people like grandparents are also precious to Him. Children who are handicapped and can't walk are very important to God. He loves everyone. Life is a gift from God, and only God can take life away.

Your Turn

1. What does God think when you hate someone? How is that like murdering someone?
2. How should you treat those who might hate you and are mean to you?

Prayer

Dear God, thank You for every life. I pray that murder will stop and people will start loving each other. Teach me not to hate others. Amen.

TV Kindness

Draw pictures inside the TV of people whose lives are important to God, or draw a picture of a news program where people are showing love and kindness.

God's Rules

God loves teamwork.

You shall not commit adultery.

Exodus 20:14

Be True When You Marry

"Let's let Becky be our team leader," said the girls on the volleyball team. Becky said she would be the leader.

When Becky told the girls where their places were on the team, one girl said, "Not me! I quit unless I can keep the score card."

Another girl said, "I quit unless I can play at the net."

One girl joined another team because she wanted to be the server.

No one wanted to be true to the team unless they had their own way. They wanted to be on the team, but they only wanted to do what they wanted to do. They weren't faithful and committed to the team.

Committed means to be true. Committing to something means not quitting when things don't go your way. A husband and wife team is God's plan for families. God wants husbands and wives to stay on the same team. God's plan is for husbands and wives to be committed to each other.

When you are grown up and get married be sure it is to the person whom God wants you to marry. Then you and your husband will be a team that stays together. The Bible says you shall not commit adultery. Leaving a husband or wife for another person is called adultery. If you get married someday, God wants you to stay on that team and not quit.

Your Turn

1. Why did God give us this rule?
2. Why did the girls above leave the team?
3. What does it mean to be committed to someone?

____

____

____

____

____

____

Prayer

Please help me to be true to family and friends. Help me to pick friends who love You and are faithful to You. Amen.

Team Work

Draw a picture of yourself on the team below to remind you that God wants husbands and wives to stay on the same team.

God's Rules

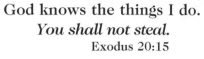

God knows the things I do.

You shall not steal.

Exodus 20:15

Keep Only What Is Yours

Kim and her mother were shopping for Christmas gift wrap. Kim saw a pretty decoration for the Christmas tree.

She said, "Mommy, look at the shiny red ball. It would look awesome on our tree. Can we buy it?"

Her mother answered, "No, we have enough tree decorations." But Kim really wanted the shiny red ball. She kept begging her mother to buy it for her. Her mother kept telling her no.

When Kim's mother went to the checkout, Kim went back to the decoration aisle. She looked up and down the aisle. There was no one around. Kim quickly slipped the ball into her coat pocket and walked back to the checkout area.

God's Word says that stealing is wrong. Kim's mother found the decoration when Kim tried to place it on the tree and she was punished. It is very hard to steal and get away with it.

God knows when you do wrong and you will usually get caught. Remember: God loves you. He will forgive you when you say you are sorry.

You wash your hands to clean them before you eat. In the same way you can also keep your hands clean for God by not stealing.

Read about a man in the Bible who used his hands to take money from people. He met Jesus and saw that stealing was wrong. He was sorry and God forgave him. (Luke 19:1-10)

Your Turn

1. Is there ever a good reason for stealing?
2. What do you think Kim's mother did when she found the decoration?
3. Why is it wrong to steal?

____

____

____

____

Prayer

God, I am thankful for Your loving kindness. Teach me Your ways. Teach me not to steal from anyone. Amen.

Clean Hands

Part of keeping your hands clean is washing them. Another way you can keep your hands clean is by not stealing. Draw your hands in the sink to show God that you want to keep your hands clean from stealing. Write "I will not steal" on the clean towel below.

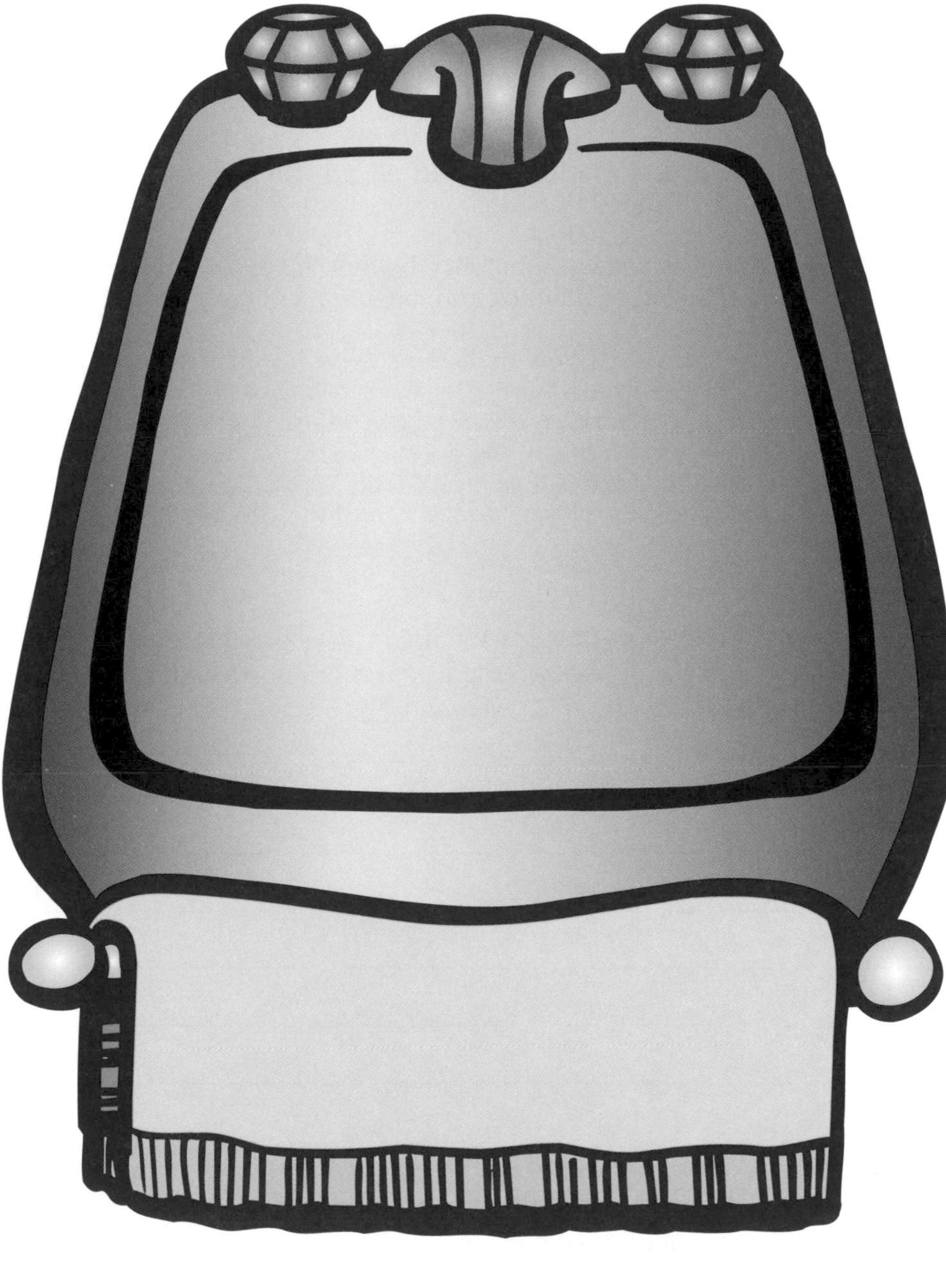

God's Rules

God wants me to tell the truth.

You shall not give false testimony against your neighbor.

Exodus 20:16

Be Honest

"Guess what she said. Let me tell you what she did. Do you know what I heard about her?"

Two girls sat in the corner of the classroom laughing and talking about Carrie. Carrie was quietly doing her math lesson. One girl laughed and said something about Carrie's mother. The other girl listened and joked even though it wasn't true. She even added something to the false story.

Have you heard people talk about someone like these girls were talking about Carrie? Carrie must have felt very badly. She didn't know what the girls were saying. They were pointing and laughing. They were telling a false story about her.

One of God's rules says you shall not give a false testimony against your neighbor. That is what these girls were doing. They were giving a false testimony against Carrie. A testimony is telling about something you know about. These girls didn't know about Carrie or her mother. Lying about others and saying things that aren't true is sin. Talking about other people in this way does not please God. It only hurts people.

Your Turn

1. What would you say to the girls talking in the corner?
2. What does God think about lying to parents and friends?
3. Is it all right to tell a lie if it is a small one?

____

____

____

____

____

____

Prayer

Please let my heart know when I tell even a small lie. Give me courage to stand up to false stories about people. Help me to never give a false testimony about someone. Amen.

Mouth Examples

You should always let your mouth be an example to others by telling something good and truthful about people. Do not use your mouth for lying. On one mouth below, tell something good and truthful about someone you know. Write a promise to God that you will not lie on the other mouth.

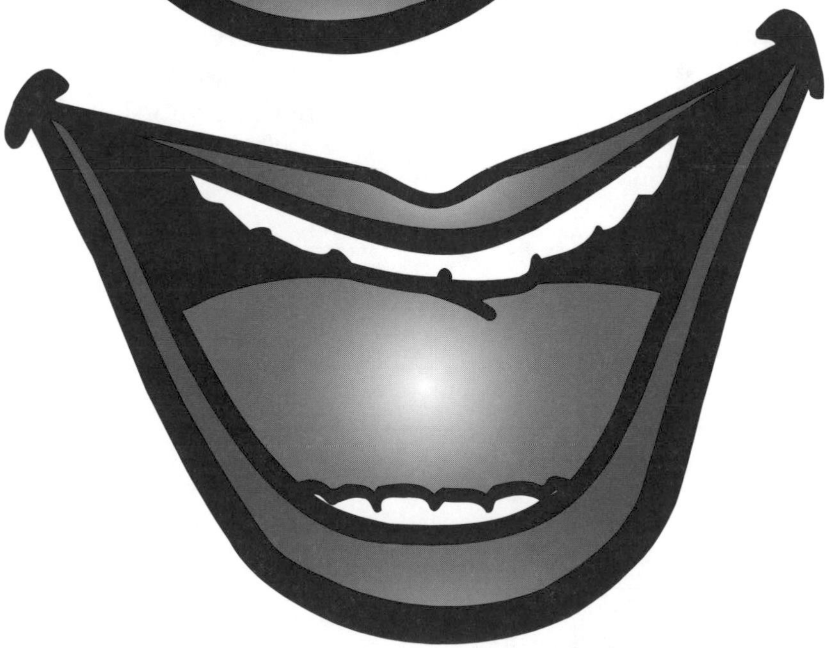

God's Rules

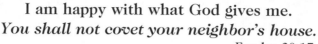

I am happy with what God gives me.
You shall not covet your neighbor's house.
Exodus 20:17

Want Only What Is Yours

Patty could stand in front of the monkey cage for hours. Monkeys were her favorite animals in the zoo.

Once she got to watch the monkeys eat their lunch. The zoo keeper slipped the food onto the cage floor. One monkey grabbed some food and climbed the tree in her cage. She put an orange under her arm and jammed two bananas into her mouth. She seemed afraid that other monkeys would get part of her food.

A head of lettuce and some mangoes were also on the cage floor. The monkey climbed down the tree and picked up the mangoes. When she saw the lettuce, she put down the mangoes and picked up the lettuce. She grabbed the mangoes again and darted up the tree. The monkey was selfish. She had stuffed so much food into her mouth at one time, she couldn't enjoy eating it.

The rule "you shall not covet" means not to want more and more. The monkey wanted more and more fruit. Be happy with what God gives and how much He gives. Wanting more and more will only make you unhappy. The monkey couldn't enjoy the food because she had too much. What about you? If you want something and you are willing to hurt someone to get it, stop. Pray and ask God if you really need it.

Your Turn

1. How do you know you are wanting something you shouldn't have?
2. What can you do when you feel you want what someone else has?
3. Is wanting something always bad?

Prayer

Dear God, help me not to want everything I see in ads on TV. Teach me not to be wanting like the monkey. Show me how to love You and be happy with what I have. Amen.

The Monkey Cage

There are two monkeys in the cage. One wants more and the other is satisfied. Color the monkey who is satisfied. Put fruit and vegetables in the cage with the monkey who wants more. Which monkey is happiest?

God's Rules

I love God with all my heart.

Love the Lord your God with all your heart and with all your soul and with all your mind.

Matthew 22:37

Little Packages

Mindy loved helping her father pick strawberries. She and her father would fill strawberry baskets to the brim.

They lined up the full baskets on the kitchen counter. The strawberries were then washed and made ready to package.

Mindy counted out ten of the biggest strawberries she could find. She put ten strawberries together in each bag. All ten in one bag made a nice package.

Jesus also put together a nice package of rules when He said this: "Love the Lord your God with all your heart and with all your soul and with all your mind."

Loving God with your heart, soul and mind makes you want to follow His rules. Do you know God?

Your Turn

1. How can this rule help you with other rules?
2. What does it mean to love God with heart, soul and mind?

____

____

____

____

____

____

____

____

____

Prayer

Lord, thank You for all Your rules and Your great love for me. Amen.

Packaged Strawberries

Can you remember God's rules for girls? Fill in the missing words on the strawberries below. The answers are on page 232.

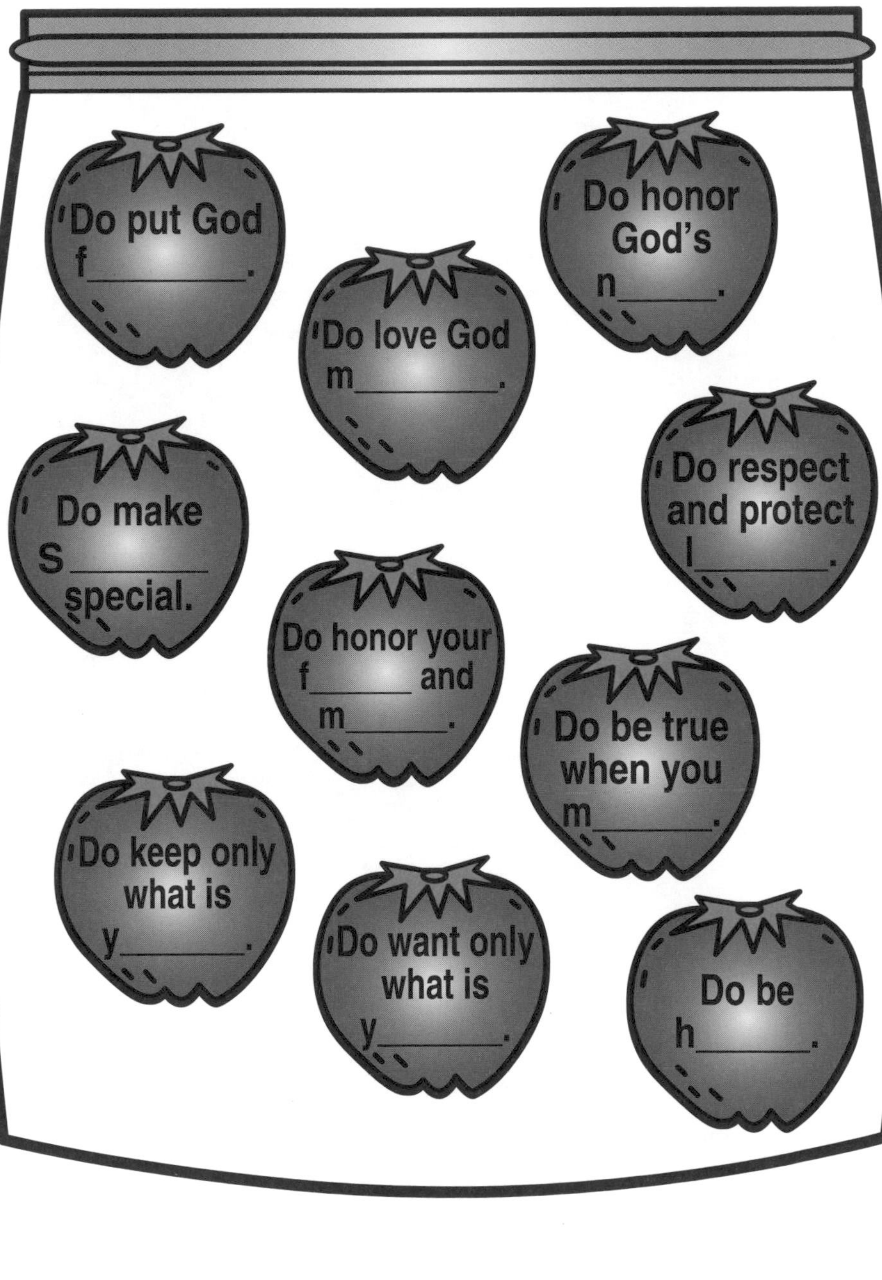
Do put God f______.
Do honor God's n______.
Do love God m______.
Do make S______ special.
Do respect and protect l______.
Do honor your f______ and m______.
Do be true when you m______.
Do keep only what is y______.
Do want only what is y______.
Do be h______.

Women in the Bible

Abigail

God cares about how I treat others.
Clothe yourselves with compassion (and) kindness.
Colossians 3:12

Abigail's Kindness

Have you ever met someone who had pretty hair, nice eyes and the best clothes? Her clothes were probably clean and stylish with matching hair bows and shoes. A person can look good on the outside, but act mean and be unkind to others. Looking good on the outside doesn't mean you are good on the inside.

David, a man in the Bible who loved God, met a woman who was beautiful outside and inside. Her name was Abigail. David hid with his men in a special place as they were running from King Saul. Abigail and her husband, Nabal, were nearby taking care of sheep.

David asked Abigail's husband for food. The rude and unkind man became angry and refused David. Abigail heard about her husband's unkindness. She loved God and had a kind heart. Abigail brought food and water to David and his men. She knew how to clothe herself with kindness inside and out. She was kind and beautiful on the inside.

God cares about how you treat people. He wants you to treat others with kindness as Abigail treated David. You can read about Abigail in 1 Samuel 25.

Your Turn

1. How can you show others you are beautiful on the inside like Abigail?
2. What could Abigail do to help her husband to be kind?

Prayer

Dear Lord, show me how to be beautiful and kind on the inside. Help me treat others with kindness like Abigail. Amen.

Abigail's Kindness Key

The underlined words below tell about Abigail's inner kindness and beauty. Look at the key. Write the word on Abigail's clothing at the right, then color the picture.

KEY

1. Abigail was sweet.

2. Abigail was thoughtful.

3. Abigail was friendly.

4. Abigail was helpful.

5. Abigail was nice with her words.

Abigail

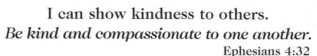

I can show kindness to others.

Be kind and compassionate to one another.

Ephesians 4:32

I Can Show Kindness

"Erin, did you finish cleaning up the dinner dishes?" asked Josh. "I think Mom and Dad asked you to do that chore. You can't watch your TV show until you do the dishes."

"Aw, shut up, Josh," said Erin. "I'm tired of you always bossing me around. I hate Mom and Dad's date night because I have to hear you."

Just then the phone rang. It was Grandma calling.

"I want to talk to Gram, I miss her so much," said Erin.

"Get on the other line," said Josh.

"How are you, Erin?" asked Gram.

"Fine," said Erin. "Except I have to do the dishes because of mean Josh."

"Oh, so you don't like Josh telling you what to do?" asked Gram.

"No, and I told him to shut up. He is a stupid brother."

"Well, Erin, I haven't heard 'shut up' or 'stupid' for a long time," said Gram. "I wonder what your mom and dad would say about those words? What does God think about it, Erin?"

"I guess I was a little unkind and unfriendly," said Erin. "Shut up isn't kind, is it, Gram?"

"No, Erin, it isn't," answered Gram.

"Gram, it's really hard to be nice when you have an older brother."

Gram told Erin how the Bible says to be kind to one another. She also told Erin to ask God to forgive her and to tell Josh she was sorry. Words like "stupid" and "shut up" were not heard again at Erin's house.

Your Turn

1. Why were Erin's words so unkind?
2. What could Erin have said instead of "shut up" and "stupid"?
3. Why does God hate unkindness?

____

____

____

Prayer

Please forgive me, God, for my unkind words. Make me more friendly and kind to people. Help me be kind to the people in my home for You and Jesus. Amen.

House of Kindness

God helped Erin to say kind words. He can help you learn to use kind words in your house, too. In the house below, draw a picture of how you can show kindness to your family, or write words of kindness in each room window.

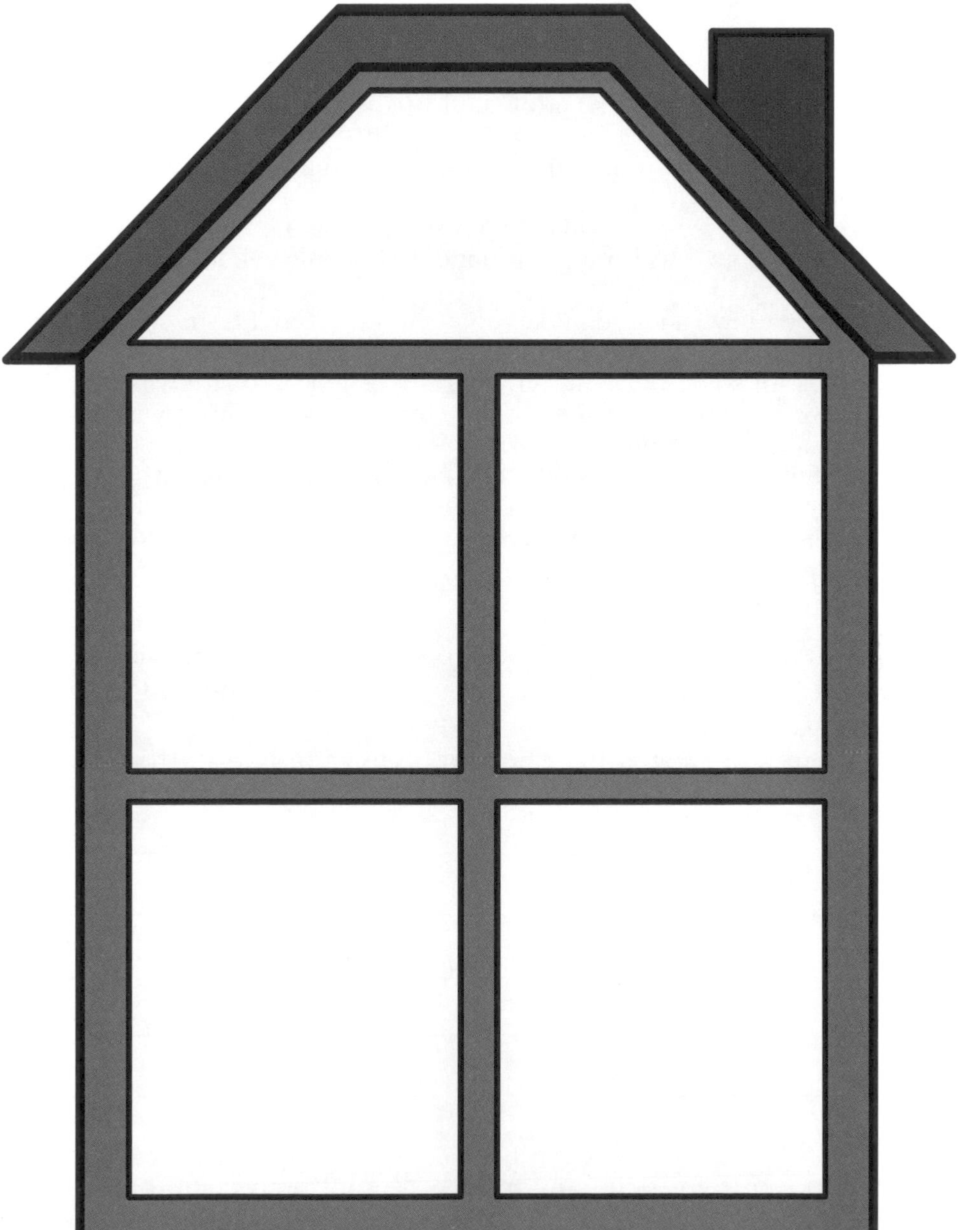

Ruth

God loves faithfulness.

Well done, good and faithful servant! You have been faithful with a few things.

Matthew 25:21

Ruth Was Faithful

Do you have a best friend? The Bible says that Naomi and Ruth were friends. They moved to Israel after their husbands died.

Ruth could have gone home after her husband's death. Instead, she moved to a strange town to help Naomi, her husband's mother. She didn't want Naomi to be by herself.

Ruth made a special promise to Naomi. She said, "Where you go, I will go. Where you stay, I will stay. Your land and people will be mine and your God will be my God."

Ruth didn't have a job to make money to buy food. So she went into the field where the farmers were cutting grain.

"I'll pick up some of the left-over grain," she said. Ruth was surprised when Boaz, the owner of the field, spoke to her. Bowing down with her face to the ground, she listened.

"Your husband died," he said. "You left your mother and father to come here with your mother-in-law. You came to a land where you didn't know anyone. The Lord your God will reward you for being faithful to Naomi."

Your Turn

1. Do you have a friend like Naomi to whom you are faithful?
2. Would you like Jesus to tell you, "Well done, good and faithful servant?"
3. How can you show others how to be faithful like Ruth?

____

____

____

____

____

Prayer

Thank You, Lord, for being my friend. Teach me to be faithful to my family. Amen.

My Promise Scroll

Ruth made a special promise to be faithful to Naomi. She didn't write her promise on a scroll, but you can. Fill in the promise scroll below by writing down the name of the person to whom you will be faithful.

Ruth

God's faithfulness helps me to be faithful.

I thank Christ Jesus our Lord...that he considered me faithful, appointing me to his service.

1 Timothy 1:12

I Can Be Faithful

"Wake up, Kathy," said Mom. "You can't sleep on the floor in Beth's bedroom."

"But, Mom, she has been sick all day," Kathy yawned. "I just want to stay with her in case she needs something. I know she would sleep in my room if I were sick."

"You are such a faithful big sister, Kathy," said Mom. Kathy should have been in her own bed. But she was being faithful to her little sister.

Are you faithful to your family and friends like Kathy? Did you know that God will always be faithful to you? When you are willing to stay close to Him, being faithful is easy. The faithfulness of God can help you to be faithful to your friends and family.

Your Turn

1. How does falling asleep on Beth's floor show that Kathy is faithful?
2. Whom can you start showing faithfulness to?
3. Why does God want you to be faithful?

Prayer

God, help me be loyal to people I know and love. Thank You for being faithful to me. Amen.

Faithful Blackout Game

How can you show you're faithful to God? Black out with a dark crayon the pictures on the quilt that DO NOT show faithfulness to God. Use a light colored crayon to color over the pictures that DO show faithfulness to God.

Naomi

I can count on God's servants.
Let love and faithfulness never leave you.
Proverbs 3:3

Naomi Was Counted On

You count on your parents for food, clothes and a place to sleep. To learn to read, write and add numbers, you count on teachers.

Ruth, a young woman in the Bible, counted on an older woman, Naomi. Ruth's parents were back at their home in Moab while Ruth lived with Naomi in Bethlehem. Ruth couldn't count on her parents at that time for food or shelter. She chose to stay with wise Naomi who had put her trust in God.

Many of Naomi's friends and family could count on her wise words. Ruth counted on Naomi's words to help her make wise choices. Naomi helped Ruth meet and marry a man named Boaz. That was a wise decision because Boaz and Ruth became the great-grandparents of King David, a great leader for God.

You should count on the good and faithful servants of God, like Naomi.

Your Turn

1. God wants you to be counted on by others. Why?
2. Whom do you count on?
3. How does God show you He can be counted on? Do you count on Him each day?

____

____

____

____

____

____

____

Prayer

Dear God, I want to be someone whom friends can count on. Teach me to be like Naomi. Show me how I can count on You each day. Amen.

A Countable Heart

Naomi had a faithful servant's heart that could be counted on for help and wise words. Do you have a faithful heart that can be counted on? What can your friends and family count on from you? Give your faithful heart to someone. Fill out the heart below. Tear out the page and give it to a friend or family member.

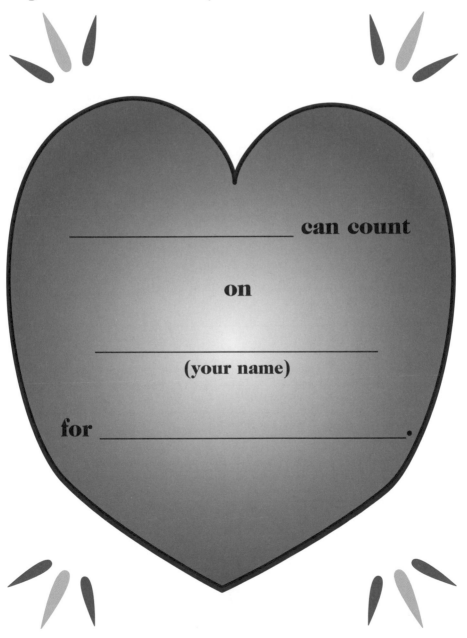

______________________ can count

on

____

(your name)

for ______________________.

Naomi

I can count on God to always be there.

We know and rely on the love God has for us.

1 John 4:16

God Can Be Counted On

"Hello, Kim? This is Keisha. Want to come over?" Keisha asked. "We should practice our three-legged race for track day at school."

"Sure," said Kim.

Then Keisha asked, "Will you listen to me recite my poem for the contest?" "Yes!" replied Kim. "You can count on me."

"I know I can always count on you!" said Keisha.

Keisha knows her friend Kim will be there when she needs help. She also knows that Kim will do what she says she will do. God is like that! He does what He says He will do, like forgive you when you do wrong. God also hears and answers your prayers the way He thinks best. You can count on Him to always be there for you.

Your Turn

1. Who counts on you?
2. How can you show friends you can be counted on?
3. How can you help others count on God?
4. How can you show God that you count on Him?

Prayer

God, I want people to be able to count on me. Show me how I can be counted on by others. Amen.

Three-Legged Race Maze

Begin at the starting line with your crayon. Put an X on the sack of the team you think is Keisha and Kim. Draw a line along the path until you get to the finish line. Win the three-legged race as a reminder that you can be counted on by others. The solution is on page 232.

Deborah

I can be a leader for God.

In your unfailing love you will lead.

Exodus 15:13

Deborah Leads

When you think of a courtroom, you probably think of a judge. The judge in court sits behind a big desk called a bench. Before God gave Israel a king, they were ruled by judges. They ruled the land in times of peace and war.

There was a wise woman judge named Deborah. She judged under a tree called the Deborah Palm. Deborah was the only woman judge in the Bible. She was a great leader who was always ready to lead for God.

The name Deborah means "see-er." God showed her many things about the people of Israel. She was a leader who lived during bad times. Israel was under the power of some evil people. With Deborah's leading, Israel's army had a mighty win over them.

Deborah sang a special song to God about the success of the army. Many gifts of music were used by her to cheer the people.

Deborah loved God and wanted to lead for Him. Are you a leader for God like Deborah?

Your Turn

1. Do you know the talents you have? How can they be used by God to lead?
2. Do you lead people toward God or away from God? How?
3. How can leading help others?

____

____

____

____

____

____

____

Prayer

Thank You, God, for being my leader. Help me lead like Deborah. Teach me to see how I can help others. Amen.

My Palm Tree

Deborah sat under her tree and listened to sad and happy stories from people. She led the people in many ways. Deborah loved God and wanted to lead for Him. How can you be a leader in school and at home? Name your own palm tree and draw yourself under it. Let the palm tree remind you that God wants you to be a leader for Him.

Deborah

God helps me to be a leader.

Teach me your way, O Lord; lead me in a straight path.

Psalm 27:11

I Can Lead

Three girls were in-line skating down a winding stone path. They came to a fork in the path. (A fork is a place where another path appears.) Peering down the new path, they saw a dark forest with many trees. Never having been down that path before, they wondered where it would lead.

Maybe it was a short cut back to their houses, they thought.

"It could lead to the park," said one of the girls.

They had been on the main path many times and had never seen the fork. The main path went by the park and back to their houses.

"Which path should we take?" they asked each other.

"Someone has to be the leader and decide," said one of the girls.

"I will," said a girl named Clara. "Let's go down the new path. I like a little adventure," she said. "Come follow me."

The other two weren't sure. Clara wanted them to do something unsafe. Sometimes others want to lead you the wrong way. You can always say no and do what is safe and right. That is what the other two girls did.

Your Turn

1. Can you think of a time when you were led to do the wrong thing? Tell your parents about it and ask them what you can do next time.
2. How can God help you to lead the right way?
3. How can you be an example for others to lead the right way?

____

____

____

____

____

____

____

Prayer

Please, God, teach Your way. Lead me down a good path so I can lead others. Amen.

Right Paths

Color the pictures at the end of each road. Circle the letters and signs at the roads God wants you to take. Draw a line from START along the right paths.

Esther

God helps me to be brave.
Be strong and courageous (brave).
Deuteronomy 31:7

Esther Was Brave

Did you ever pretend to be a queen? Esther was a real queen! In Bible times, Esther was queen in a place called Persia. She loved God.

The king of Persia saw Esther's beauty. He made her the queen but he didn't know that she was a Jew. That means she was one of God's special people.

Haman, a man second to the king, wanted to get rid of Jews. Esther heard of evil Haman's plan. If his plan worked, Esther's family and friends could die. She might even be put to death.

The queen knew she should tell the king about Haman's plan. But Esther was only allowed to talk to the king if he sent for her. If she asked to see him, the king could have her killed. So Esther prayed and she told her friends and family to pray for three days.

After three days, Esther made a special dinner for the king and evil Haman. The king was so pleased that he told her she could have anything she wanted.

Esther said to the king, "My king, I hope you are pleased with me. If it pleases you, let me and my people, the Jews, live."

When the king found out about Haman's wicked plan, he had him killed. Esther and her people were saved because she chose to be brave. Esther asked God to help her be brave and He did. He will help you to be brave, too.

Your Turn

1. Could you have done what Esther did?
2. Does God have any special jobs for you where you need to be brave?

____

____

____

____

____

Prayer

Dear God, I trust You to help me be brave just as You helped Queen Esther. Give me a brave heart like Esther. Amen.

Queen Esther's Code

Can you find a message in Esther's crown? Use the numbers on the crown to read Esther's secret code. Write each letter on a line below. The answers are on page 232.

__ __   __ __ __ __ __ __   __ __ __

2 5   19 20 18 15 14 7   1 14 4

__ __ __ __ __ __ __ __ __ __

3 15 21 18 1 7 5 15 21 19

__ __ __ __ __ __ __ __ __ __ __ 31:7

4 5 21 20 5 18 15 14 15 13 25

Esther

God is with me when I am afraid.
Do not be afraid, for I am with you.
Genesis 26:24

Living God's Way

Have you ever felt like shadows were dancing everywhere in your room? It can look like every wall in your room has shadows: a monster dances on the window drape or big, scary spiders dance behind the hanging plant.

Shadows and frightening sounds are everywhere! Dark rooms can be scary. But shadows cannot hurt you. There's nothing to be afraid of, but sometimes you can still be afraid. God wants you to be brave and call on Him for help.

One way to show you are brave is to pray. When shadows begin to dance, you can ask God to come and calm you. Dancing shadows aren't real, but God is. God wants you to know that He is bigger than shadows dancing on walls.

The next time you are afraid, ask God to help you to be brave.

Your Turn

1. What should you do to show bravery when you're afraid?
2. How can you make shadows go away?

____

____

____

____

____

____

____

____

____

Prayer

God, help me to be brave when I see shadows at night. I know they aren't real, so teach me to pray. Amen.

Shadow Prayers

Write I WILL BE BRAVE inside the shadow. When you are brave and pray, the shadows go away.

Esther

God can make me strong and brave.
Do not be afraid or discouraged (sad).
2 Chronicles 32:7

I Can Be Brave

Has anyone ever made fun of you?

Maybe they said something like this: "Look at that girl! What is that book she is carrying? It looks like a Bible. How weird she looks with that book. She must be one of those Jesus people. A goody girl or something."

That is a girl who is brave for Jesus. She stands up for what is right and true. A girl who loves God must be brave and hold her head high.

The Bible is the true Word of God and is a very special book. There are people who like to tear down the things of God. It hurts when people tease you because of what we think and believe. But God can make you strong and brave if you ask Him for help. When someone tries to take away what you believe, you can sing a song to help you be brave. Sing this to the tune of "Mary Had a Little Lamb."

Jesus helps me to be brave,
To be brave,
To be brave.
Jesus helps me to be brave,
So I won't be afraid.
He is with me every day,
Every day,
Every day.
He is with me every day.
He will make me brave.

Your Turn

1. Has anyone ever made fun of you for something you ever said or did for Jesus? What did you do?
2. When you think of being brave, do you think of fighting a war?
3. How is being brave by carrying a Bible to school like fighting a war?

____

____

____

Prayer

Dear God, please help me to be brave when someone teases me. Help me to be brave and stand up for what is right and good. Amen.

War Medal

When men and women do something great in a war, they get a medal. Being teased because you love Jesus is like getting a medal in heaven. Decorate your own medal below for being brave for Jesus.

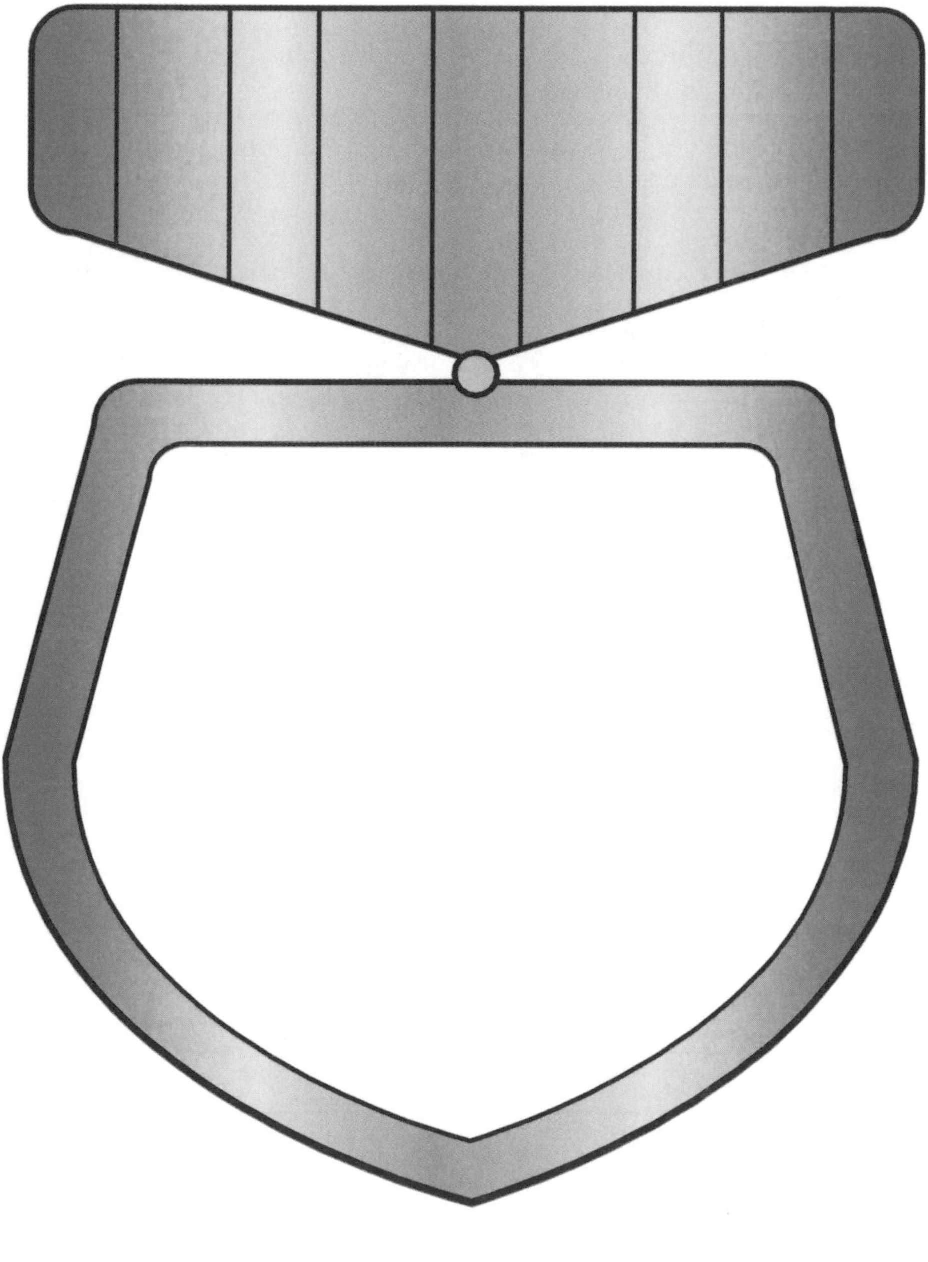

Hannah

God hears and answers my prayers.
My house will be called a house of prayer for all nations.
Isaiah 56:7

Hannah Prayed

Hannah was a woman of prayer. She and her husband traveled miles from home to pray in the house of prayer.

Hannah spent hours praying in the holy tent of God. She was sad because she couldn't have a baby. She cried as she prayed to the Lord.

One day, Hannah made a promise to God. She said, "Lord, the Powerful One, don't You see my sadness? Please don't forget me. If You give me a son, I will give him back to You all his life."

Hannah had prayed so hard from her heart that her mouth moved, but there was no sound. God heard her prayers and He answered her. Later, she gave birth to Samuel, a strong son.

Hannah kept her promise to God. When Samuel was old enough, Hannah took him back to the same house of prayer. He stayed there to learn how to do God's work.

Like Hannah, you are heard by God when you pray with all your heart. Hannah knew God and she knew how to pray.

Your Turn

1. Why do you think Hannah stayed so long in the house of prayer?
2. Why did Hannah believe that God would answer her prayer?
3. Do you think God will answer your prayers?

____

____

____

____

____

____

____

Prayer

Thank You, God, for listening to my prayers. I know You hear my prayers as You heard Hannah years ago. Help me trust You each day. Amen.

House of Prayer

Follow the numbers around Hannah and put her in God's house of prayer.

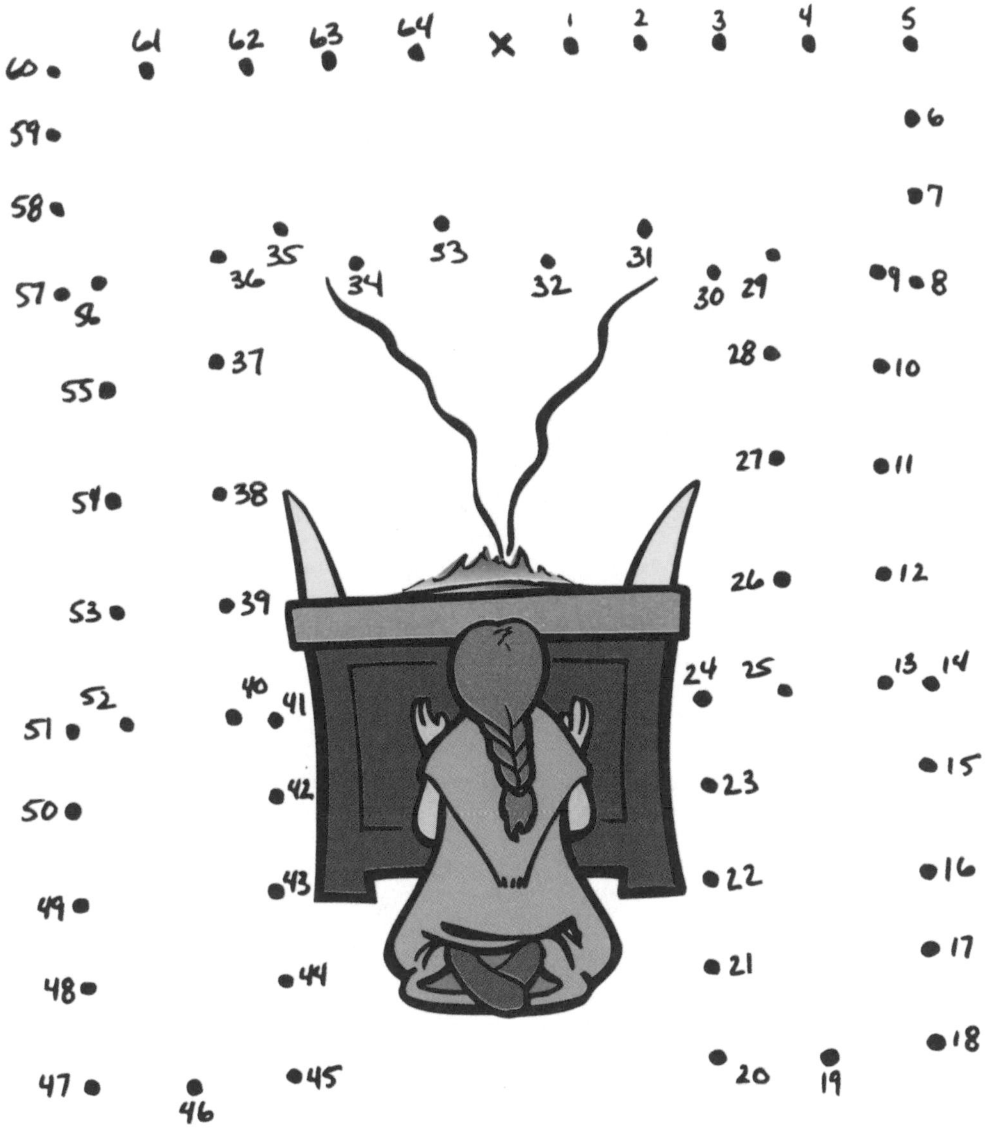

Hannah

God wants to talk to me each day.

When you pray, go into your room, close the door and pray to your Father...in secret.

Matthew 6:6

I Can Pray

"How was school today, Tina?" asked Dad as the family sat around the dinner table one night.

"It was pretty good," answered Tina while she picked at the food on her plate. "I found a great place to pray at school. It's on the playground,"

"On the playground?" asked Dad.

"Yes," said Tina.

"How can you pray on the playground?" Dad asked in a surprised voice.

"It's crowded there and no one notices when I pray," said Tina. "Plus, there's always something to pray for there. Kids get hurt all the time. They fall off the monkey bars or skin their knees playing ball!"

Tina sounded excited as she shared about her new place of prayer. "Today, I saw a boy hitting another boy," she said. "He had to sit down the rest of the recess. I prayed God would help him learn that hitting isn't the way to solve problems."

"Then while I was swinging, I thought of the Shank family. I know they are moving to Israel next month to be missionaries. I asked God to help my friend Anna adjust to a new life, far from here."

Dad spoke up, "That just goes to show you, prayer is good anywhere and anytime. Jesus said, 'Go into your room, close the door and pray to your Heavenly Father.' You can pray anywhere and anytime without anyone knowing."

Tina's dad is right. If you pray with your brain and not your mouth, that is like praying in secret. Playground prayer is as good as praying in your secret prayer place.

Your Turn

1. Why did Jesus say to pray in secret?
2. Does it matter to God where or when we pray?
3. Can you think of a new place where you can pray?

Prayer

I thank You that I can talk to You anytime and anywhere. Show me the people around me that I can pray for. Teach me to pray always. Amen.

Playground Prayer

Write on the playground the names of people you know who need prayer, then color the picture.

Dorcas

I can put others first.

In humility consider others better than yourselves.

Philippians 2:3

Dorcas Put Others First

Dorcas loved Jesus! She was the only woman ever called a disciple. Another word for "disciple" is "follower" of Jesus.

Dorcas lived in a town named Joppa near where Jesus had lived. She liked to sew for poor people. Dorcas didn't have a husband. Her husband had died, so she was called a widow.

Dorcas's life was spent thinking of others before she thought of herself, just like Jesus did. Doing God's work and helping people made her happy. One day, Dorcas got sick and died. Other widows washed her body and placed it in an upstairs room in her house. Friends were very sad that Dorcas had died.

Peter, a friend and disciple of Jesus, heard Dorcas died. He went to the upstairs room where Dorcas was laid. Widows stood around her crying and looking at the robes and clothes Dorcas had made for others.

Peter sent everyone out and said to Dorcas, "Get up." She opened her eyes and, seeing Peter, she sat up. Peter called all her friends back into the room. They were so happy! Dorcas was able to spend many more years putting others first.

Your Turn

1. What made Dorcas put others' needs ahead of her needs?
2. What can you do to help others and put them first?

Prayer

Teach me, dear God, to care about other people. Help me to put the needs of others ahead of mine. Thank You for women like Dorcas, who cared enough to help people. Let me be like Dorcas. Amen.

Good Works Fabric

Dorcas did good things until the day she died. One of her good works was sewing clothes for poor people. Can you think of ways you can do good works by putting others first? Write or draw a pictures of them below on the bolts of fabric.

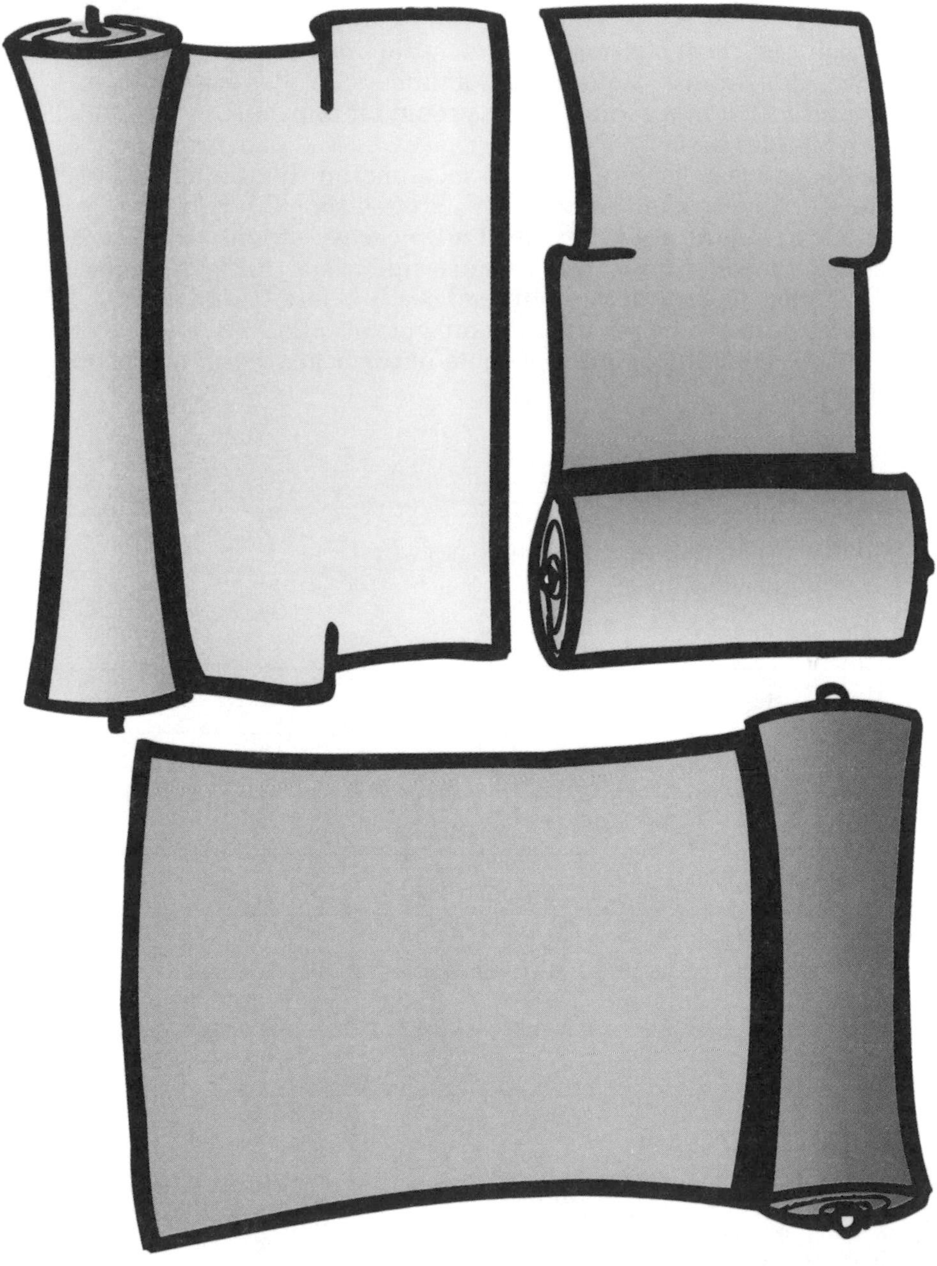

Dorcas

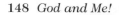

Jesus always put others first.

Honor one another above yourselves.

Roman 12:10

I Can Put Others First

Two girls arrive at a fast food stand at the same time. Who should order first? Two girls wait the same length of time for a roller coaster ride. When time comes to get on the ride, there is room for only one. How should they decide who rides first?

Your mom asks for your help in cleaning up the dinner dishes. Your favorite TV show is about to begin. Which one should you do first?

Choosing to put others first isn't always easy. If you aren't sure what to do, ask yourself a question, "What would Jesus do?" The answer will usually be that Jesus would put others' needs before His own.

Letting others be first in line and putting others ahead of yourself pleases God. Thinking of other people's needs before your own is one way to be happy.

Your Turn

1. Why should we put others first?
2. What can you call not putting others first?
3. Do you put God first?

Prayer

Dear God, help me to remember to put other people first. I want to do what Jesus would do. Thank You, God, for putting me first with You. Teach me to put You first, God. Amen.

WWJD Hidden Puzzle

Can you find and circle the words, "What Would Jesus Do?" They are hidden in the letters below. The answers are on page 232.

Q	R	K	W	I	J
S	L	M	H	M	E
Z	F	P	A	Z	S
W	U	O	T	O	U
W	O	U	L	D	S

The Lost Coin

God is pleased with a happy heart.
A happy heart makes the face cheerful.
Proverbs 15:13

A Happy Woman

Jesus told stories to teach people about His love. Here is one that He once told.

There was a woman with ten silver coins. People worked many hours to earn just one coin. The woman wasn't careful with her coins and lost one of them.

"Oh, no!" she sighed. "What did I do with that coin of mine? I will have to clean the house and look in every cupboard and closet."

The woman began to clean her house. She turned over every piece of furniture. Suddenly, she found her lost coin. It was a wonderful surprise to her. She was so happy that she called all her friends and told them what had happened.

"I had ten silver coins and I lost one. I was so sad and worried. I found the coin when I cleaned out my house," she said. "I'm so happy. Please be happy as I'm happy."

The Bible says, "A happy heart makes the face cheerful." The woman had a cheerful face when she found her coin.

Your Turn

1. What makes you happy? Should you share what makes you happy with others?
2. Does knowing Jesus make you happy? Should you tell someone you are happy because you know and love Jesus?

____

____

____

____

____

Prayer

Thank You, Jesus, for loving me. Your love makes me happy. Teach me to tell others about Your love so the angels in heaven can celebrate. Amen.

Angel's Coins

Write the names of children you know who need to hear about Jesus inside the coin. Plan to share the good news of Jesus with them.

The Lost Coin

Knowing God makes me smile.

Is anyone happy? Let him sing songs of praise.

James 5:13

I Can Be Happy

"Mother! Mother!" cried Amanda as she came running into the house from playing outside.

"What is it, Amanda?" Mom asked.

"Grumpy Mr. Ginn chased Abby and me out of his yard," Amanda answered. "He said it is a home for special birds and we were scaring them away. We weren't doing anything, just walking across his yard. He acts so grumpy and he never smiles."

"Well, maybe you had better stay out of his yard," said Mom.

"Mom, do you think Mr. Ginn is happy inside?" Amanda asked. "He sure doesn't look happy outside."

"You can tell when people are happy inside because they usually have a smile on their faces. It's hard to say with Mr. Ginn because we don't see him everyday. Only God knows what's in his heart for sure," said Mom. "The Bible tells us in Psalm 4:7 that God filled David's heart with joy. Just knowing God loved him made David happy."

Mom hugged Amanda and said, "God loves us, too. He loves us so much that He let His only Son, Jesus, die on a cross for our sin."

Mr. Ginn didn't seem to know how much God loved him. When you are happy, you should smile and sing praises to God.

Your Turn

1. What makes you grumpy? How can God help you smile?
2. How do you know God loves you?
3. How can you help "grumpy" people be happy?

____

____

____

____

____

Prayer

Dear God, help me to remember that You love me, so I can be happy on the inside. Amen.

Happy Faces

Put an "S" by the faces that show sadness, "H" by faces that show happiness and a "G" by the faces that look grumpy. Draw your own happy faces at the right. When you know the love of God, you smile and sing praises.

Lydia

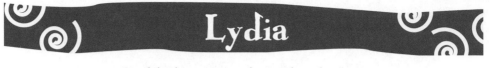

God helps me make right choices.

Show me your ways, O Lord, teach me your paths.

Psalm 25:4

Lydia Chose God's Way

In Bible times, travelers could ask anyone along the road for a place to sleep at night. Even a stranger! People who loved God offered food and shelter for each other as they traveled from town to town.

A woman named Lydia loved everyone she met. Lydia owned her own business. She sold purple cloth and purple dye. Since purple was a wanted color in Bible days, Lydia became rich. Travelers liked staying in her big home.

One day Lydia and her friends gathered at the river to pray to God. A man of God named Paul stopped at the river to tell the people about Jesus. Lydia hadn't heard about Jesus. She didn't know that He died for sins.

Lydia listened to God's ways as Paul talked. That same day, Lydia and her family were baptized in the river. She wanted to show others that they were happy to know Jesus.

Lydia decided to live God's way. God helped her make the right choices in selling cloth. Lydia asked Paul and his friends to stay at her home.

Paul and his people stayed with her. Lydia loved God and chose to do things His way.

Your Turn

1. How can you choose God's way, like Lydia did, and help others?
2. Would you let someone in need stay in your room?
3. Lydia was a business woman who sold cloth. What do you think God wants you to do when you grow up?

____

____

____

____

____

____

Prayer

God, help me to choose God's way in everything I do, like Lydia. Help me to listen and learn about Jesus every day. Amen.

Adopt a Family

Lydia always helped others and invited them to stay at her house. Ask your parents if they know any poor families who might need help. Ask if you can "adopt" this poor family. At Christmas and birthdays you can take them toys. You can take groceries to them at Thanksgiving. If you can't find a poor family, adopt a neighbor and take cookies to them. Fill out the adoption papers below and begin helping others.

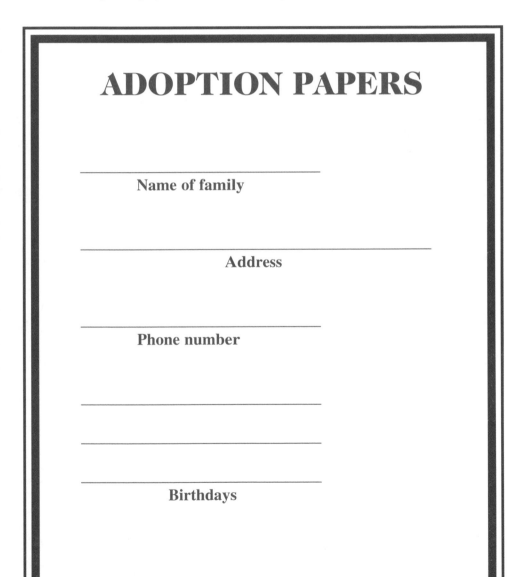

ADOPTION PAPERS

____

Name of family

____

Address

____

Phone number

____

____

____

Birthdays

Lydia

I will choose God's way.
Find out what pleases the Lord.
Ephesians 5:10

I Can Choose God's Way

"No school lessons for two weeks! Vacation is finally here," said Tasha.

"There are always lessons to be learned, Sweetie," said Dad.

"Like what?" asked Tasha.

"I know a lesson that is easy to know about, but hard to do," said Dad.

"Tell me, Dad," replied Tasha.

Dad got his Bible and looked up a verse in the New Testament. "The Bible says we should find out what pleases God and live His way," he said.

"Is that the lesson?" asked Tasha.

"Yes!" answered Dad. "First, we need to learn what pleases God and then we choose God's way. It pleases God when we choose to obey our parents. It pleases God when we choose to help others. It also pleases God when we put others first. What do you think about the lesson so far, Tasha?"

"I already do those things, Dad," said Tasha.

"Are you sure?" asked Dad. "Do your mouth and ears always choose God's way? Do your hands choose God's way? Do your feet choose God's way? Do you know what pleases God well enough to do things His way?"

"I see what you mean, Dad," said Tasha. "I want to learn more about what pleases God. With God's help, I will choose His way."

"That's my girl, Tasha," said Dad.

Your Turn

1. Why is it hard to choose God's way?
2. Think of ways to please God and choose His way with your mouth, feet and hands.

____

____

____

Prayer

God, help me know what it means to choose Your way. Help me to do it. Amen.

Just Do It!

Read about pleasing God in Ephesians 5:10 of the Bible. Can you just do it and choose God's way? You will need these words to solve the puzzle: hands, feet, mouth and ears. The answers are on page 232.

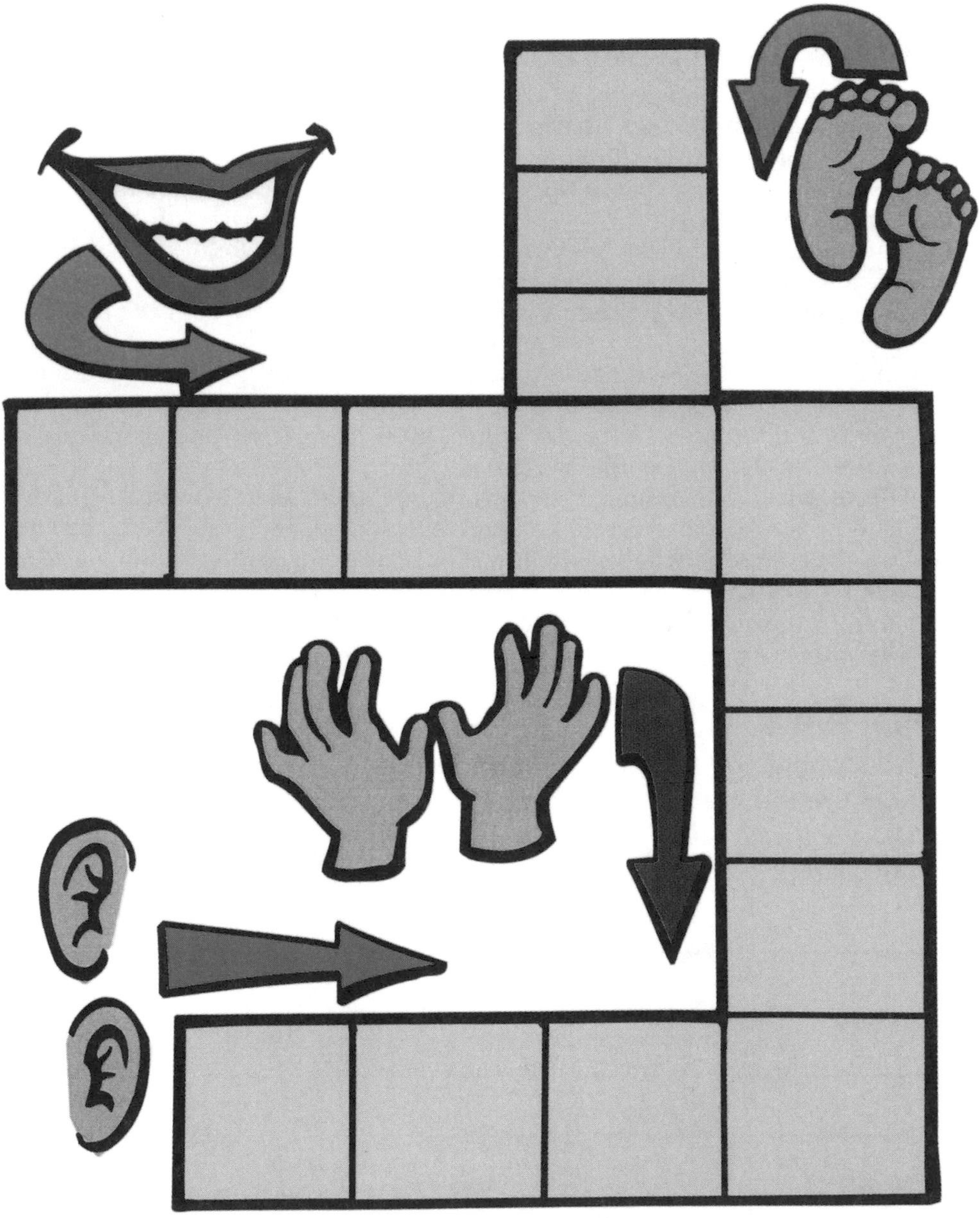

Sarah

I can follow God.

I am the Lord your God...who directs you in the way you should go.

Isaiah 48:17

Sarah Followed God

Do you know the meaning of your name? In the first lesson you learned that names have meaning. Remember Sarah, the one whose name means "princess"? Sarah knew how to follow God. She and her husband, Abraham, lived a happy life in the city of Ur. God provided a nice home and everything they needed.

One day, Abraham came home from working in the field. He had some special news for Sarah! An angel had appeared to him in the field that day. The angel said, "Leave Ur and move your home to a new country built by God."

Sarah listened as Abraham told her the angel's message. She could have asked, "What place is this? How long will we be there? What about leaving my friends and my pets?" But she didn't, even though she had grown up in Ur and Ur was the only home she knew.

The angel told Abraham they would not even have a map to follow. "Just follow God's voice," said the angel. Sarah had many questions and no answers. But, she knew how to follow God. Sarah knew that following God sometimes means not asking questions.

Could you learn like Sarah to trust and follow God's way no matter what He tells you to do?

Your Turn

1. How would you feel if your family had to move? Could you follow God even if you weren't happy about moving?
2. Do you think you love God enough to follow Him like Abraham and Sarah?

____

____

____

____

Prayer

Dear God, I want to be a follower of You, like Sarah. Teach me to trust You as Sarah did. Amen.

Following God Bag

God tells us to follow Him. Following God's voice meant Sarah had to move from her home to a strange place. What does following God mean you should do? Write your ideas on Sarah's bag. Pray and ask God to help you do these things and follow Him.

Sarah

God wants me to follow His ways.

The ways of the Lord are right; the righteous walk in them.

Hosea 14:9

I Can Follow God

Have you ever sat next to people in school who do not follow the leader? Instead of following the teacher and copying spelling words from the chalkboard, they make paper airplanes.

Have you sat behind people in church who do not follow the pastor's sermon? Instead of following along, they color on their church bulletins.

What about at home? Have you ever played with your fork instead of following Dad or Mom at dinner time prayers?

Notes must be followed carefully to play a song on the piano. In dancing you must follow the teacher's steps to learn the dance. If you start the dance too early or end too late, the dance will be wrong.

Following God's way is like taking the right dance steps to make a beautiful dance. God wants you to follow Him so your life will come out right.

The Bible says, "The ways of the Lord are right." You do wrong when you forget to follow God's ways. You can start to follow God by reading the Bible and going to church. Talking to God in prayer also helps you follow Him. Then you have joy and happiness.

Your Turn

1. Why should you follow your teachers, parents and pastor?
2. How can you follow God by leading others?
3. Think of a time when you didn't follow at school, home and church. What can you do to begin following the right way?

____

____

____

____

____

____

Prayer

God, help me to learn to follow You at school, home and church. Show me how to follow You so I can live Your way. Amen.

Dancing Shoes

Following God's way is like making the right dance steps in a beautiful dance. On the dance shoes below, write or draw pictures of different ways to follow God at school and at home.

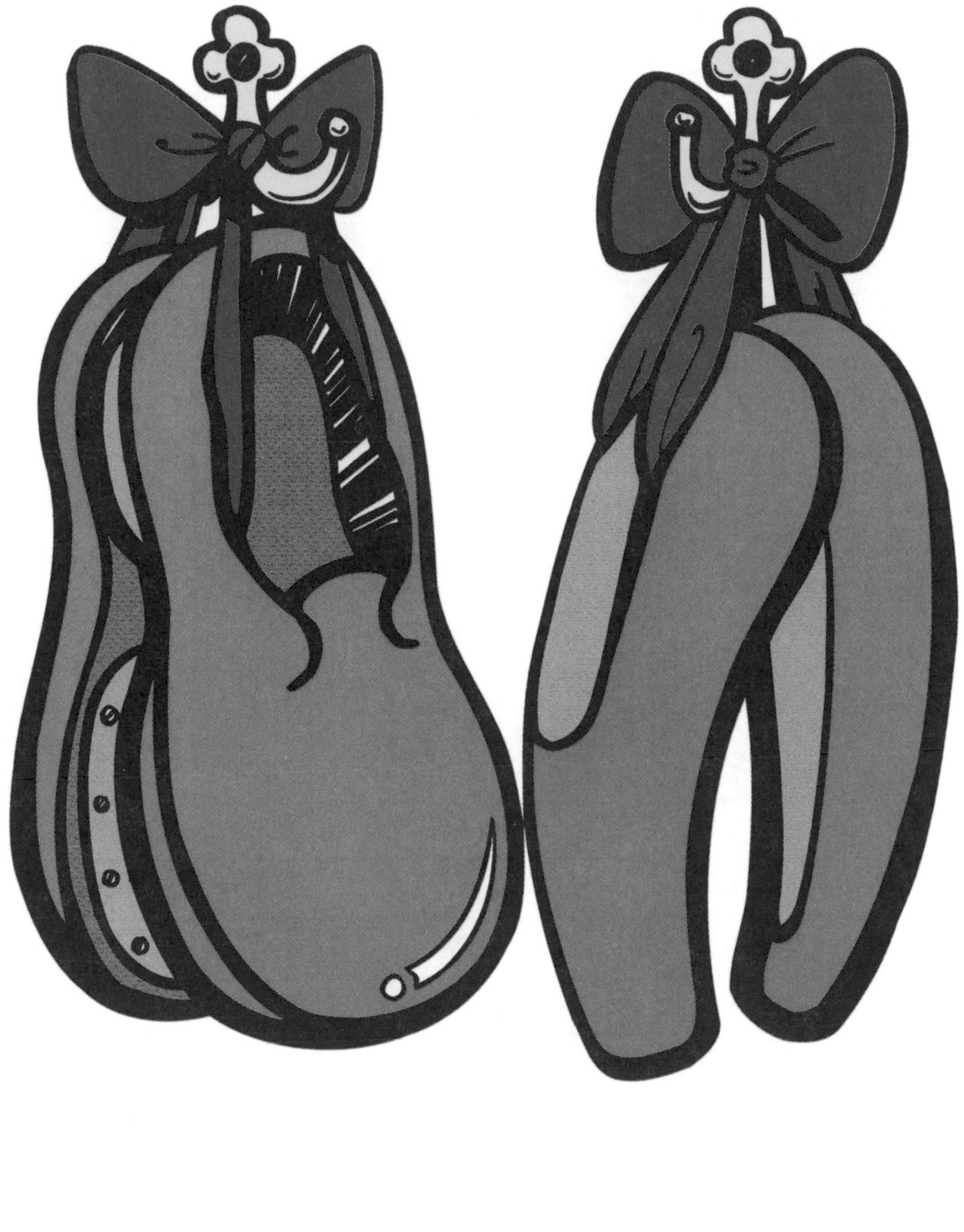

Phoebe

I will look at the ways of Jesus.
My eyes are ever on the Lord.
Psalm 25:15

Phoebe's Eyes Were on Jesus

A woman in the Bible named Phoebe fixed her eyes on Jesus her Lord. Watching what Jesus had done showed her how she should act.

A missionary named Paul liked Phoebe. Missionaries are people who go around telling others about Jesus. She had done things to help him in his travels.

Phoebe took a secret note to a church in a place called Rome for Paul. His letter told the people in Rome to welcome Phoebe. It said to take care of her because she was a deacon in the church.

Deacon means "servant." A deacon is someone who helps others at the church in special ways. Phoebe may have cleaned up dishes after church meetings or she may have sewn for the poor in her town.

Paul always said good things about her to others. He said in Romans 16:1-2 that Phoebe had been a great help to many people.

Phoebe always kept her eyes on Jesus. That's what made her care more about others than herself.

Are your eyes like Phoebe's? Are your eyes always on Jesus?

Your Turn

1. Why do you think Phoebe helped others?
2. How can you tell Phoebe kept her eyes on Jesus?
3. How can you keep your eyes on Jesus?

Prayer

Dear God, teach me to help others. Let my eyes start seeing people who need help like Phoebe did. Help me keep my eyes on You, Jesus. Amen.

Seeing Jesus

Draw a picture of your eyes on the top half of this page to remind you to keep your eyes on Jesus. On the bottom half write the Bible verse. Tear it out of the book and give it to someone special.

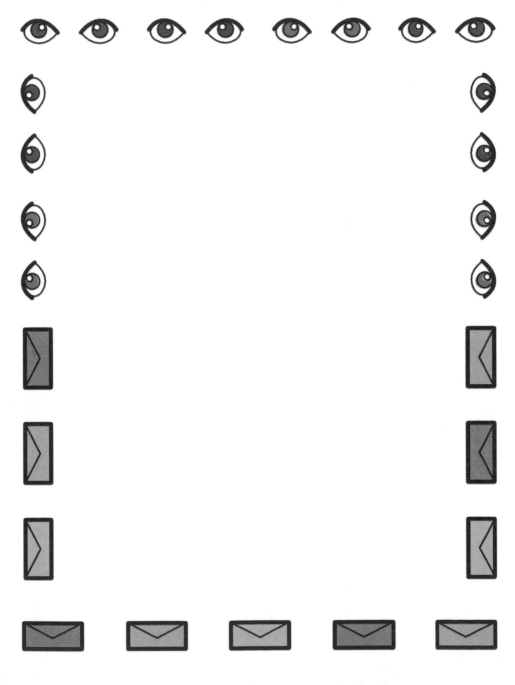

Phoebe

I can keep my eyes on Jesus.
Let us fix our eyes on Jesus.
Hebrews 12:2

Looking the Right Way

What do your eyes see each day? Do they see TV or video games?

A girl named Sam didn't keep her eyes on Jesus. Her eyes were on herself. "Sam, Mrs. Lamp next door needs someone to play with her 3-year-old daughter while she does her baking. She's making bread for the sale at the homeless shelter," said Mom.

"Oh, do I have to?" asked Sam. "Sally is coming over to play and I don't want to."

Mom answered, "Sam, you need to give your time to Mrs. Lamp. You can play dolls with Sally any day. Mrs. Lamp needs your help today." Mom told Sam that by helping Mrs. Lamp she would also be helping women and children at the shelter.

When your eyes are on Jesus, you will want to help others because Jesus helped others. Your grandfather may need his house cleaned. A friend's cat may need to be fed while she is away on a trip. A sick person in the hospital may need prayer. Eyes that are on Jesus find helping others easy.

Your Turn

1. How do people know if your eyes are on Jesus?
2. How do you know if God wants you to give someone your time?
3. How does giving your time to others make you feel?

Prayer

God, help me to be ready to help others. Show me people who I can help. Amen.

Know Your Verse!

Follow the directions below.

Learn the verse

Hebrews 12:2
Let us fix our eyes on Jesus.

Know the verse

Do the dot-to-dot below using the words of the verse.

Write the verse

Write the verse on the lines below.

☆ ______________________________

♥ ______________________________

Think about this

If you want to learn to live God's way, you must attend church, read the Bible and obey His words. Do you know Jesus as your Lord and Savior?

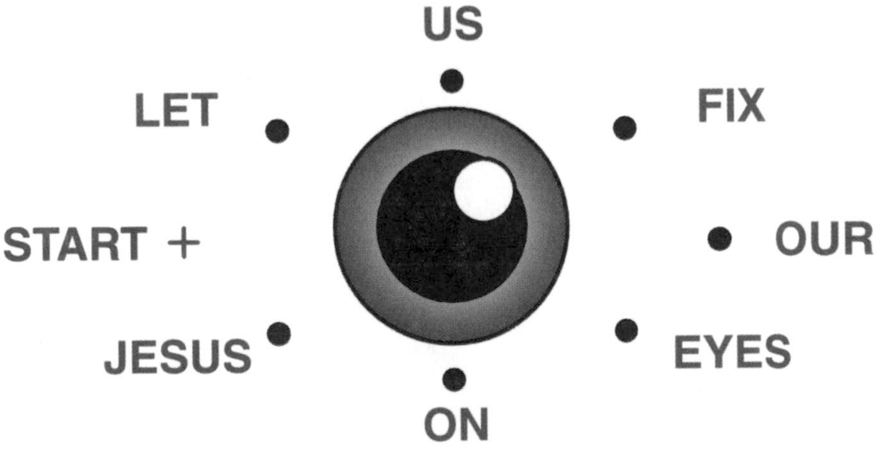

Miriam

I thank God each day.
Praise the Lord, for the Lord is good.
Psalm 135:3

Miriam Thanked God

"Sing to the Lord for He is good!" shouted Miriam.

Aaron's sister Miriam was a woman who loved to worship God. She was called a "hearer" of God's Word. God told her many special things to tell the people.

Once, God split the sea and made a wall of water. The wall stayed on both sides as Moses held his hand out toward the sea. The people of Israel took their goods and walked across the sea bed onto dry land. They were running from the mean king of Egypt. He had set the people of Israel free from slavery, but changed his mind.

God's people got to the other side of the sea in time. The waters went back onto the king's army. The king's horses, chariots and horsemen went into the sea and were killed.

When Miriam saw how God had helped them, she was very thankful. She took a small drum with bells and danced before the Lord. Many of the women followed her as she sang a song of thanks to God. The song was like this: "Sing to the Lord for he is good. The horse and its rider he has cast into the sea." It was a song of thanks for God's success over the bad king. Miriam thanked her God. Read about Miriam in Exodus 15:20.

Your Turn

1. Name some things for which God deserves your thanks.
2. What should you do when you are thankful to God?
3. Do you thank God often enough? What can you do to thank Him more often?

Prayer

Thank You, Lord, for the times You have helped me. Thank You for taking care of me. I will sing praises to Your name, for You are a good God. Amen.

Music Puzzle

Miriam took a drum with bells on it and danced before her people and the Lord. Try to read the letters on each bell tied to the drum. Place a letter on the matching numbers below the drum to write a message. If the number on a bell is 1, write the letter on line one, and so on. What is the message you read on the lines? Can you sing and dance before the Lord? Do it! The answers are on page 232.

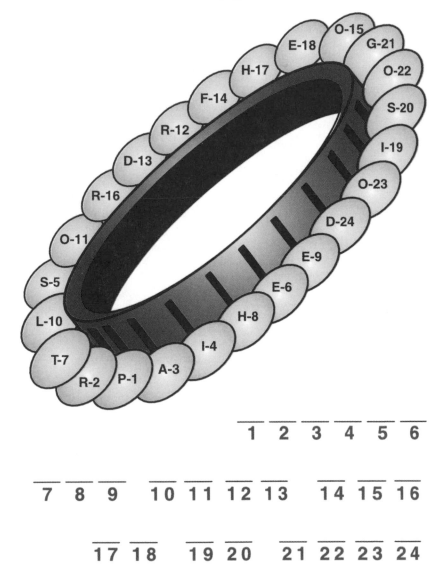

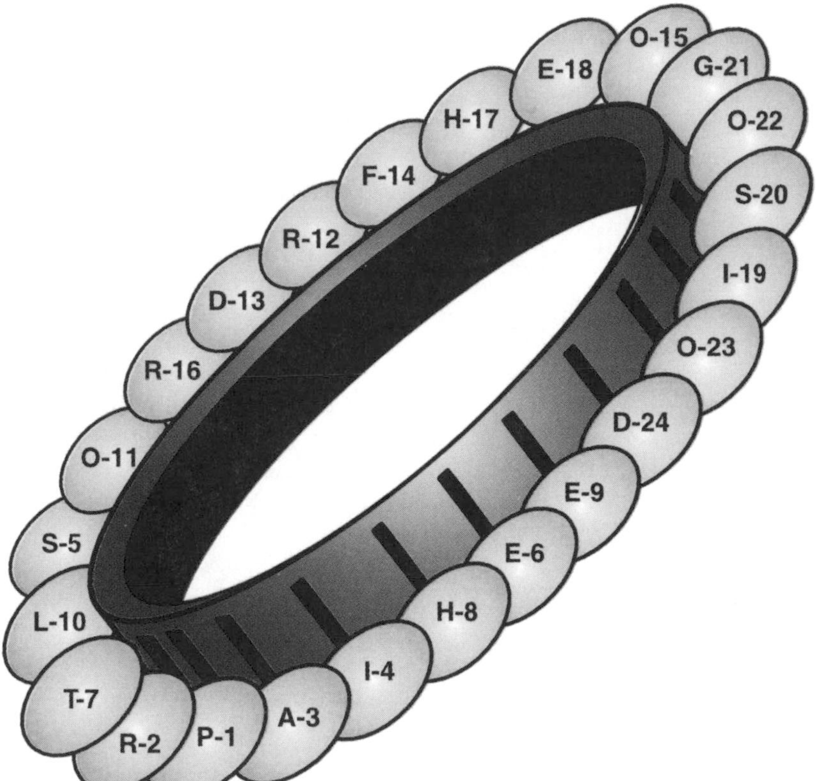

__ __ __ __ __ __
1 2 3 4 5 6

__ __ __   __ __ __ __   __ __ __
7 8 9   10 11 12 13   14 15 16

__ __   __ __   __ __ __ __
17 18   19 20   21 22 23 24

Miriam

I will give thanks every time.

Praise the Lord, O my soul, and forget not all his benefits.

Psalm 103:2

I Can Thank God, Part One

"Guess what happened," said Mom.

"What?" asked Carey.

"Mrs. Dever told me Ruthie ran her bike into the big tree at Goliath Hill. She got going too fast and couldn't stop. Luckily, she wasn't hurt too bad because she wore her helmet. Mrs. Dever said she only had a scrape or two. It could have been a lot worse. Isn't God great to have kept her from harm?"

"Yes," answered Carey. "I ride my bike over that hill almost every day. I've never run into that tree."

Mom smiled. "I guess we tend to forget when God protects us until something happens like with Ruthie. We only want to give thanks when something bad almost happens."

"Maybe we should thank God more that we aren't hurt," said Carey.

"The Bible says to give thanks in all things. So even bad things can be a blessing to the people of God. We should never forget all His benefits to us and give thanks every time." Mom gave Carey a big hug.

Carey turned to her and said, "What a cool God we have!"

Your Turn

1. Think of some things that happened this week for which you can give thanks to God.
2. Name good things that have happened to you and bad things that have happened to you. Can you give thanks?

Prayer

Thank You, God, for all the love and care You give us each day. Thank You for being good to us even when we forget to give thanks for the good things that happen. Help me not to forget You, God. Amen.

Goliath Hill

What is your Goliath Hill? Write a letter on the hill to God. Thank Him for something new He has done for you.

Miriam

God wants me to thank Him for everything.
Always giv[e] thanks to God the Father for everything.
Ephesians 5:20

I Can Thank God, Part Two

"I don't want to take out the trash. I don't want to clean my room and make my bed. I don't want to hang up my coat. I don't want to put my bike away."

Joy was always groaning and saying, "I Don't Want" about doing chores. "You need to stop the 'I Don't Wants' when it comes to doing chores, Joy," said her mom. "God wants us to give thanks to Him for all things."

"Does that mean I need to give thanks for having to make my bed and clean my room?" asked Joy.

"There are some children who don't have their own room. The floor is their bed," answered her mom sternly.

"Well, what about the trash?" asked Joy.

"Some people bury their trash in the yard," said Mom. "We are lucky to have trash pick-up."

"Are you saying that I should thank God when I take out the trash? And I guess I should thank God when I clean my room too, huh?"

"Yes," said her mom. "You're right on both counts. The Bible says, 'Give thanks for everything.'"

Can you give thanks for the things you do not enjoy doing? Giving thanks in all things is not easy. But you will be glad you did.

Your Turn

1. Which person pleases God? The one who gives thanks in all things, or the one who groans?
2. What is the hardest thing for you to give thanks for?

Prayer

Dear God, help me to remember that You love me. Help me to give thanks in everything. I will be Your happy child. Amen.

Thank You Card

Design the front of a thank-You card to God. You should thank Him for chores and other things you do. On the front of the card draw pictures of the things you do that you need to be thankful for.

Mary, Mother of Jesus

Loving Jesus helps me love others.

Mary treasured up [saved] all these things and pondered [thought about] them in her heart.

Luke 2:19

Mary Loved Jesus

"I love you, Maddie," said Mom.

"I love you, too, Mom," answered Maddie.

Maddie's mother smiled and remembered holding and rocking Maddie when she was a baby. She had saved that memory in her heart. She loved her child and wanted to remember special times with her.

Jesus' mother loved Him, too. At Jesus's birth, Mary wrapped Him tightly in warm clothes and laid Him in a manger. She loved and cared for Him. Mary saved the memory of that night in her heart.

At 12, Jesus became lost from His family. His parents had traveled to Jerusalem for a special Jewish party. While they traveled home, they noticed He was not there. Mary and her husband went back to look for Him. After three days of much worry they found Him. Jesus was sitting in the temple, listening to teachers and asking questions. Mary asked Him why He had caused her to worry so much. She was worried because she loved Him! Mary was there when Jesus was born and she was there when He died on the cross for us. Mary loved Jesus! What about you?

Your Turn

1. What memories of love do you keep in your heart?
2. How can loving Jesus help you love others?

____

____

____

____

____

____

Prayer

Dear God, help me to love Jesus and to get to know Him more each day. I pray You will help me to love others, too. Amen.

Memories of Love

What are some memories of love you keep in your heart? Draw a picture or list them in the heart below. Let your heart memories remind you of the love Mary had for Jesus. Jesus wants your love, too.

Mary, Mother of Jesus

I can't see Jesus but I love Him.
Though you have not seen him, you love him.
1 Peter 1:8

I Will Love Jesus

Ella and her mother walked the hall at St. James Hospital looking for Grandpa's room number. Ella stopped in the middle of the hall.

"Look at this picture of Jesus on the wall, Mom. Is this what Jesus really looked like?" asked Ella.

"I don't know, Ella," she said. "Nobody really knows what He looked like. There were no cameras that long ago."

"I'd like to see Jesus and know what He really looked like," said Ella.

"Would that make you love Him more, Ella?" asked Mom.

"No!" answered Ella. "I love Him even though I can't see Him. It doesn't matter to me what He looks like, either. I know what He has done for me."

Ella's mother took her hand. "In the Bible, a friend of Jesus' named Peter said, 'You don't need to see Jesus to love Him,'" Mom said. "I am proud of you for having faith in Jesus."

Your Turn

1. What do you think Jesus looked like?
2. How can we love someone we can't see?
3. How can you show Jesus you love Him?

Prayer

I love You, Jesus, even though I can't see You. I don't need to see You to love You. I love You because You love me and died for me. Amen.

I Love Jesus Puzzle

Write the first letters of the names of the things shown in the pictures to find the message. In the small hearts, write things Jesus has done for you. The answers are on page 232.

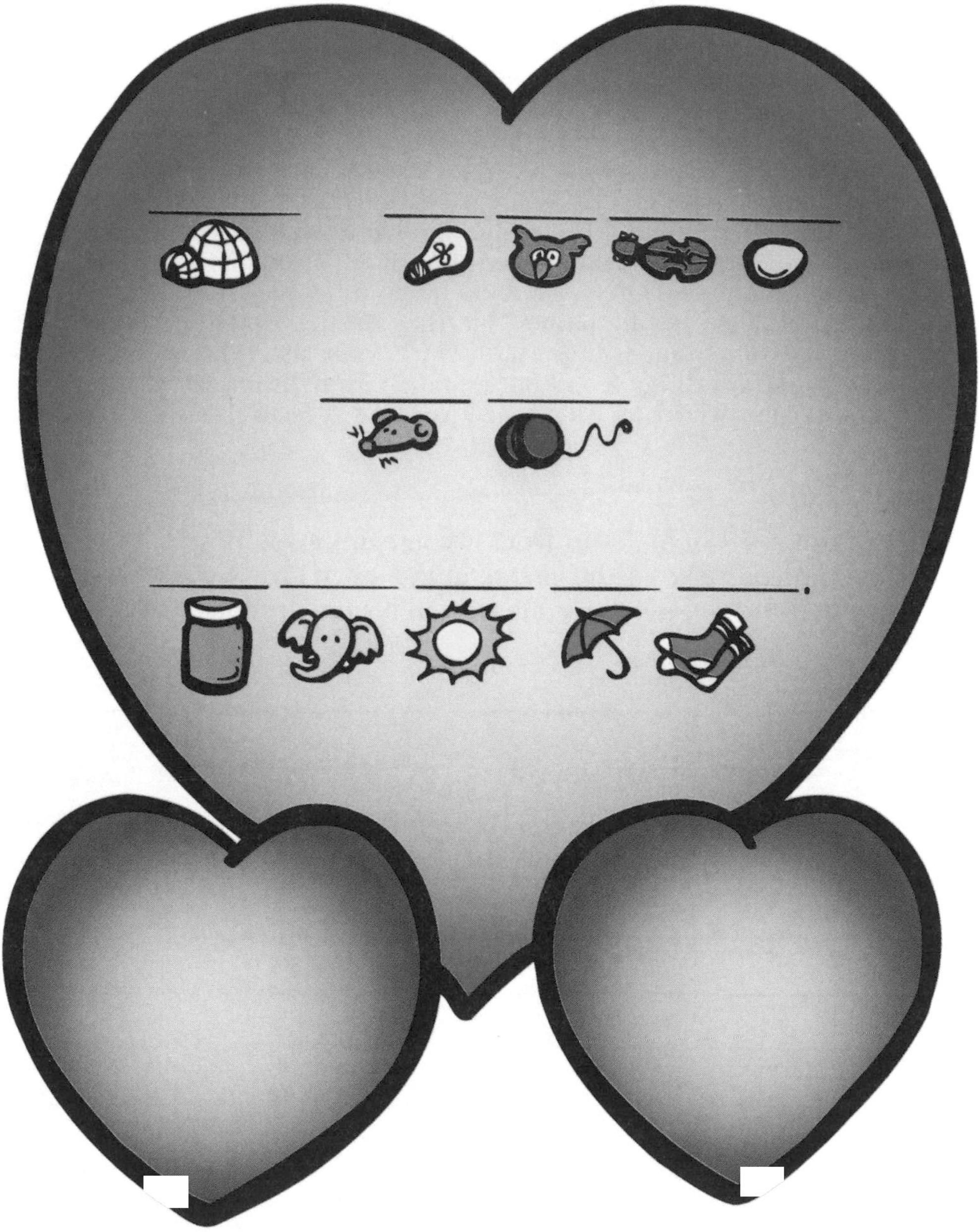

Mary and Martha

I will sit at Jesus' feet.

Do not forsake (leave) your friend.

Proverbs 27:10

Mary and Martha's Friend

Once there were two sisters who lived together. One night, a good friend came to have dinner with them. They both loved their friend very much. The sisters were always happy when this friend came to see them. One of the sisters hurried around the room to set the table and prepare the meal. She was very upset and worried about how the meal would taste.

The other sister sat quietly at the friend's feet and listened to Him.

How wise and wonderful He is, she thought as she followed every word He said. Finally, the busy sister asked the friend, "Don't You care that my sister isn't helping me? Tell her to help me!"

The guest called her by name. "Martha, Martha. You are worried and upset, but only one thing is important. Mary, your sister, has chosen to do the most important thing. It will not be taken away from her."

Can you guess who their friend was? Yes! It was Jesus. Is He your friend?

Your Turn

1. How can you "sit at Jesus' feet" if you cannot see Him?
2. How can you tell that the sisters in the story love Jesus?
3. How does the verse tell us one way to become friends with Jesus?

Prayer

Dear Jesus, thank You for being my friend. Teach me to be a good friend to others. Amen.

The Sisters' Friendship Bracelet

Trace the dotted lines below to make a friendship bracelet. Write your name on the line. Both of the sisters loved Jesus. Only one sister knew how to be a friend.

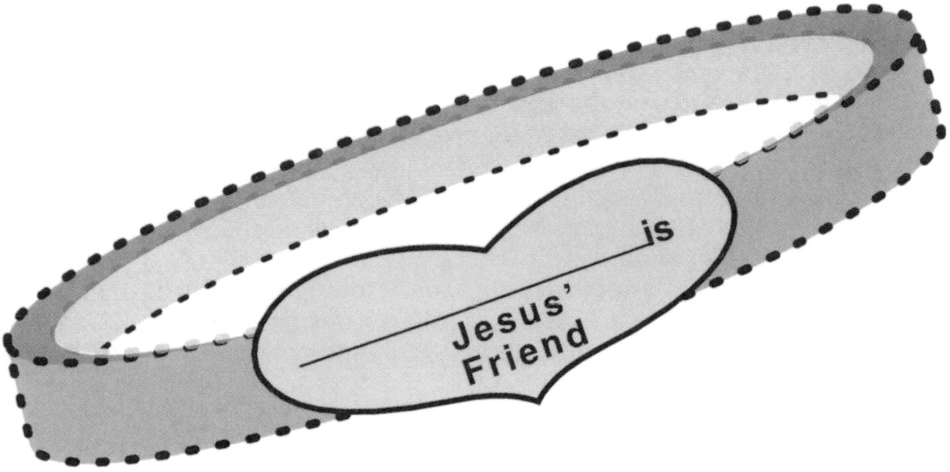

Mary and Martha

Jesus helps me love my friends.
You are my friends if you do what I command.
John 15:14

Jesus, My Friend

Tami ran to the car in tears. She climbed into the front seat and put her head in her hands.

"Tess isn't my friend anymore!" she sobbed.

"Why isn't Tess your friend?" asked Mom.

"She won't do what I tell her to do," said Tami. "I wanted her to jump rope with me at recess and she wouldn't do it. Then, she wanted me to sit by her at lunch and I wanted to sit by Casey."

"You girls usually do what the other person wants to do," said Mom. "What happened?"

Making friends and keeping them isn't always easy. The more friends do for each other, the better friends they become. Jesus said, "You are My friends if you do what I tell you to do."

What do you think Jesus wants you to do? How can you be His friend? You can't jump rope with Jesus. But you can obey your parents, help others and tell the truth. Jesus wants you to always speak kind about others and believe He is your Lord and Savior.

Your Turn

1. How can you tell when people are friends?
2. How do you think Jesus wants you to treat your friends?
3. What can you change in your life to be better friends with Jesus?

____

____

____

____

____

Prayer

Dear Jesus, I want to be Your friend and do what You want. Please forgive me for not doing what You want me to do. I want everyone to know that You are my friend. Amen.

Friendship Pages

On the friendship pages below, write on the left side how you plan to be a better friend.

Joanna

I will bless Jesus.
Praise [bless] the Lord, O my soul;
all my inmost being, praise his holy name.
Psalm 103:1

Joanna Blessed Jesus

Rowing a boat is hard work. In trying to get to the shore, you row harder and harder. You are rowing with all that is within you.

Running a race is the same way. You want to win so you run with all that is within you to the finish line.

A woman named Joanna wanted to bless Jesus with all that was within her. She was thankful to Jesus because He had healed her. Joanna and her friends traveled with Him and His disciples. She used her own money to help them buy food and whatever else they needed.

Joanna bought spices and oils to prepare Jesus' body for burial when He died. She was there with some women when His tomb was found empty. Joanna went with them to tell the disciples Jesus had risen.

With everything that was within Joanna, she blessed Jesus. When King David wrote "All that is within me, bless His holy name," he meant, "I want to thank God with everything inside me."

Do you love Jesus enough to bless Him with all that is in you? Ask God to show you how.

Your Turn

1. Why did Joanna want to bless Jesus with all that was within her?
2. Do you have reasons to bless Jesus with all that is within you?
3. How can you show Jesus you want to bless His holy name?

____

____

____

____

____

____

Prayer

Dear God, thank You for sending Jesus to die for me. Teach me to bless You and Jesus with all that is within me. Amen.

Row Your Boat

You can read about Joanna in Luke 8:2-3, Luke 23:55 and Luke 24:11. Do you have reasons to thank Jesus with all that is within you? What will you do to bless Jesus? Write your ideas on the boat oars.

Joanna

God helps us to bless others.

Let us love one another.

1 John 4:7

I Can Bless Jesus

Katie Ruff knew her Bible better than any kid in school. She attended the weekly Bible club at her church. She went to Sunday school each week, too.

Katie wanted to bless Jesus by being nice to others. But there was one girl she couldn't be nice to. That was Betsy!

Betsy had made fun of Katie's new haircut in front of other kids. She had said, "Your new haircut looks funny. I wouldn't be seen with that hair on my head." That really hurt Katie and she never forgot it. Katie wouldn't talk to Betsy or look at her. She hated her.

Hating someone doesn't bless Jesus. Blessing Jesus means to praise Him and make Him happy. Katie couldn't bless Jesus as long as she hated Betsy. One week in Bible club, Katie heard the teacher talk about love. She read from the Bible, "Beloved, let us love one another." The teacher said that loving others blesses Jesus. She also told how God sent Jesus, His only Son, to die and pay for our sins.

Katie began to think about Betsy. She thought, *If God and Jesus love us, we should love others. If I don't love Betsy, then I will not bless Jesus.*

Katie knew she couldn't say she loved God and hated Betsy. *I want to always bless Jesus and others*, she thought. At that moment, Katie asked God to forgive her. The next time she saw Betsy she said hi and was friendly.

Your Turn

1. How does hating someone make you feel?
2. If you want to bless Jesus, how will you treat others?
3. What should you do when you find yourself hating someone?

____

____

____

____

Prayer

Dear God, thank You for being so willing to forgive us. I love You and Jesus. I want to be a blessing to Jesus. Teach me to always love others so I can be a blessing. Amen.

Blessing Jesus Chart

On the pictures below, write the things you plan to bless Jesus with.

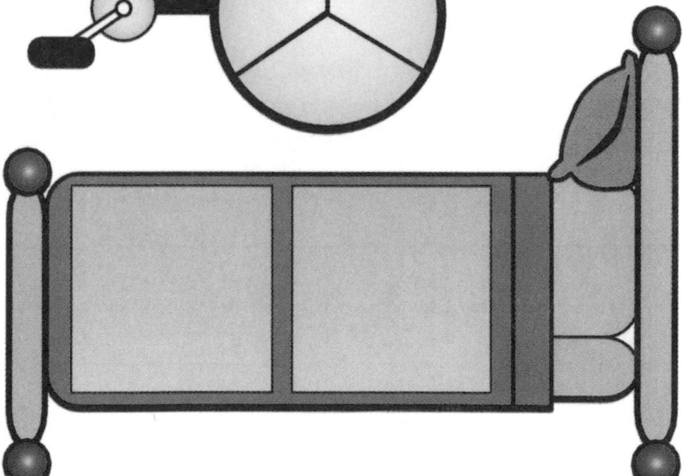

Rahab

Showing goodness helps God.
Trust in the Lord and do good; dwell in the land and enjoy safe pasture.
Psalm 37:3

Rahab Showed Her Goodness

Do you like to watch spy movies? There aren't many spy movies where a good woman is the heroine. The Bible tells a story about a good woman who helped two spies.

God's leader for Israel, Joshua, planned to take over the city of Jericho. Joshua's two best spies were sent out to Jericho to check out the city. A woman named Rahab lived in a house built on Jericho's city wall. She was a good woman.

Rahab helped the spies by allowing them to hide from the king of Jericho at her house. The spies lay down on her roof while she covered them with a plant called flax.

The king's men searched the house, but didn't find the spies. When it became dark, Rahab lowered a red rope over the wall. The men escaped as she helped them climb down the rope. The spies ran back to Joshua's camp.

Rahab's goodness was rewarded by the two spies. Rahab was told to gather her family in her house. She was to mark it by hanging the same red rope over the wall. When the army came, the good woman, Rahab, and her family were saved.

Your Turn

1. Would you risk your life to help spies for God?
2. What was Rahab's reward for doing good? What do you think your reward will be for doing good to others?
3. How can you help others to do good?

Prayer

Dear God, show me how to do good like Rahab did. Help me to do good so others will want to do good. Amen.

Goodness Rope

The Bible says, "Trust in the Lord and do good." What does it really mean to do good? Look up the word "good" in a dictionary. See the lines by the rope below? Write the words from the dictionary on the lines that tell what it is to do good. For example: "doing the right thing."

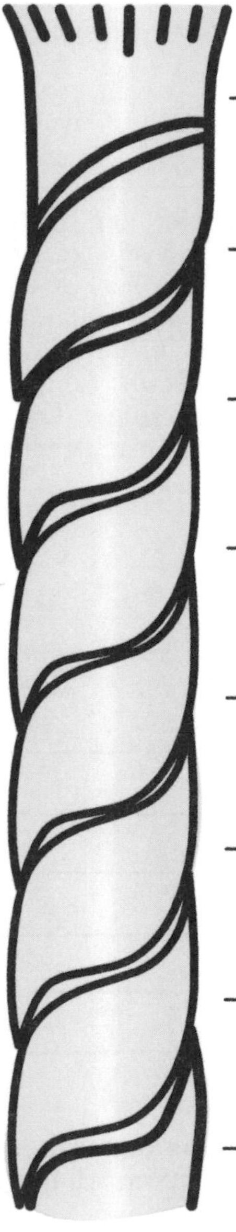

____

____

____

____

____

____

____

____

Rahab

Don't get tired of doing good.
Let us not become weary in doing good.
Galatians 6:9

I Can Show Goodness

A girl and her big brother take newspapers to sixty of their neighbors each day. They make every effort to put the papers onto the people's walkways. Most of the other paper boys and girls throw their papers from a moving car. Those newspapers land on the driveways.

But the girl and her brother want to do a good job. They want to do good and serve the people on their block. They put the papers on the walkway. How many neighbors do you think noticed and tipped them? Only four! Their neighbors do not notice their goodness.

Should the girl and her brother quit putting papers on the walks because the neighbors do not notice? It would be sad if Jesus got tired of doing good to us because we do not notice Him. We even disobey Him in different ways each day. But He keeps right on forgiving and helping us.

Jesus doesn't get tired of doing good things for us because He loves us. We shouldn't get tired of doing good things for others either. Remember, many people didn't value what Jesus did for them in Bible times. They still don't today. Jesus continues to do good anyway. He does not want us to get tired of doing good.

Your Turn

1. What good do you do that makes you tired?
2. Read about the ten lepers in Luke 17:11-19 in the New Testament of the Bible. Why did only one notice Jesus's goodness?

____

____

____

____

____

____

Prayer

Dear Jesus, thank You for loving me enough to help me even when I don't do good. Help me to do good to others and obey You. Help me to notice Your goodness. Amen.

Headline Scramble

Jesus wants you to not give up doing good to others. Try to figure out the headline for the newspaper page below. Use the happy faces below to decode the words. Write the decoded words on the lines on the front page of the newspaper. The answers are on page 232.

good become doing let of us not weary

Jochebed

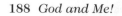

I put my trust in God.

Blessed is the man who trusts in the Lord.

Jeremiah 17:7

A Mother Trusted God

A girl got a heart locket from her father for her birthday. Her father died soon after. She was very sad, but she wore the locket to remember him. When she went to camp she had to trust her mother to take care of the locket until she returned.

Have you trusted anyone with something of value to you?

Once there was a Hebrew mother who trusted God to help her protect her baby boy. The evil king of Egypt gave orders that all Hebrew boys should be killed. The woman, Jochebed, was able to hide her precious boy for three months. After three months, she knew she would need to do something to protect her baby.

Jochebed got a basket and covered it with tar so it would float. She put the baby in the basket. Then she put the basket in the tall grass at the edge of the river. The daughter of the king came to the river to bathe. She found the basket and took the baby as her own. The princess named him Moses. Jochebed was happy that her baby was safe. Pouring her trust into God and placing him in the basket saved her baby. Can you pour your trust into God? What will you trust Him for?

Your Turn

1. Would you trust God to take care of you?
2. How can trusting God make you happy?

Prayer

Dear God, show me how to pour my trust into You each day. Amen.

Pouring Trust

Jochebed poured her trust in God into the basket with her baby. God cared for her son. Trace the trust lines from you to the basket. Pouring your trust in the basket is giving your trust to God. Write what you trust Him for in the basket.

Jochebed

God wants us to trust Him.

Those who know your name will trust in you.

Psalm 9:10

I Can Trust God

Have you ever played the blindfold game? One person is blindfolded while another person leads her around the room. The blindfolded person must trust who is leading her.

Being blind can make life hard for some. We use our eyes to do everything. But there are ways the blind can see without their eyes. The blind can learn to trust a cane to help them walk. They can learn to trust a dog or a friend to help them find their way.

Blind people can trust their noses to smell things. They can trust in their ears to hear things. They can trust in their feet and hands to help them feel things.

Many of us can see with our eyes, but we still must learn to trust. We learn to trust police to help us cross the street. We trust doctors to do what is best for us. We trust our parents to catch us when we jump into their arms from a tree. We trust our dad or mom to drive us safely to dance lessons.

God wants us to trust Him, too. God will always be with us and we can trust Him no matter where we go or what we do.

Your Turn

1. How do you show your parents you trust them?
2. Who are some people you trust the most?
3. Why should you trust God to help you?

Prayer

Dear God, I can trust many people that I can see. Help me to trust You, God, for everything. Amen.

The Blindfold

Write names of people you trust across the girl's blindfold.

The Offering

Sharing is God's way.
Be generous and willing to share.
1 Timothy 6:18

A Woman Who Shared

How do you feel when someone shares a slice of pizza with you? What about doll clothes and other toys?

It should be easy for most people to share. A poor woman in the Bible found something to share from the little bit she had. One day people with nice clothes came to the temple to hear Jesus. They didn't just have nice clothes, they were rich. While Jesus talked, these rich people walked into the temple. Everyone watched them as they went by. They wanted people to see how much money they put into the money box. They liked for others to think that they were important.

The money box was a large box where worshipers put their offering to God. After the rich people left, a poor woman quietly walked up to the money box. She quickly put in two tiny coins and left.

Jesus saw her and said to His helpers, "When this poor woman put two coins in the box, she shared more than the rich people shared." The helpers didn't understand. They had seen all the money the rich had placed in the box. How could two coins be worth more than that?

Jesus explained, "God looks at a person's heart to see why they do things. The rich people could have shared much, much more. They shared for the wrong reasons. They wanted others to think well of them. They didn't care if they pleased God. The poor woman shared everything she had because she had a great love for God."

Your Turn

1. What do you think God sees in your heart?
2. Have you ever thought you were important for doing something good?

____

____

____

____

____

Prayer

Thank You for all You give us. Teach me to save my money to share at Sunday school. Amen.

The Coin Purse Hands

A coin purse can remind you of the sharing woman in the story. She probably worked hard just to earn two coins. Draw something on the coin purse that you would like to share. How much money can you share at Sunday School or give to the poor? Write it down!

The Offering

God wants me to share with others.

Do not forget to do good and to share with others.

Hebrews 13:16

I Can Share

Della didn't like to share anything with her twin sister, Stella. But their parents didn't have a lot of money so the girls had to share some things.

The twins shared their bedroom and bathroom. Some of their clothes were shared. Their radio alarm clock and night light were shared. Della always fussed about sharing. She even drew a make-believe line down the center of their bedroom to keep Stella off her side.

Stella was very different. She loved to share her things with people. Her lunch was always shared with kids at school. She once took all of her allowance and gave it to Della to buy a new lunch box. Stella tried to share clothes with Della, but Della wouldn't. This made Stella very sad.

One day Stella got sick and went to the hospital. The doctors said she needed a certain kind of blood to help her get well. Only Della had that kind of blood. Della would do anything to help her sister get well again, even share. She told God she would begin to share with Stella if Stella could just go home. Della even took down the make-believe line in their bedroom.

Stella did get well and came home. Della told God how sorry she was for not sharing with her sister. Della was never selfish again. In fact, she noticed how much happier she felt when she shared.

Your Turn

1. Why does God want us to share?
2. Why was Della happier when she began to share with her twin sister?
3. How can you teach others to share?

____

____

____

____

____

____

Prayer

Dear God, thank You for the many gifts You give. Help me to be good in sharing what I have. Show me whom I can share with. Amen.

My Share Line

Sharing means to give. It doesn't always mean that you give to someone and they give something back. See the share line below? On one side of the line, draw pictures or write the names of people you should be sharing with at school, home and church. On the other side of the line make a list of things you can share with God.

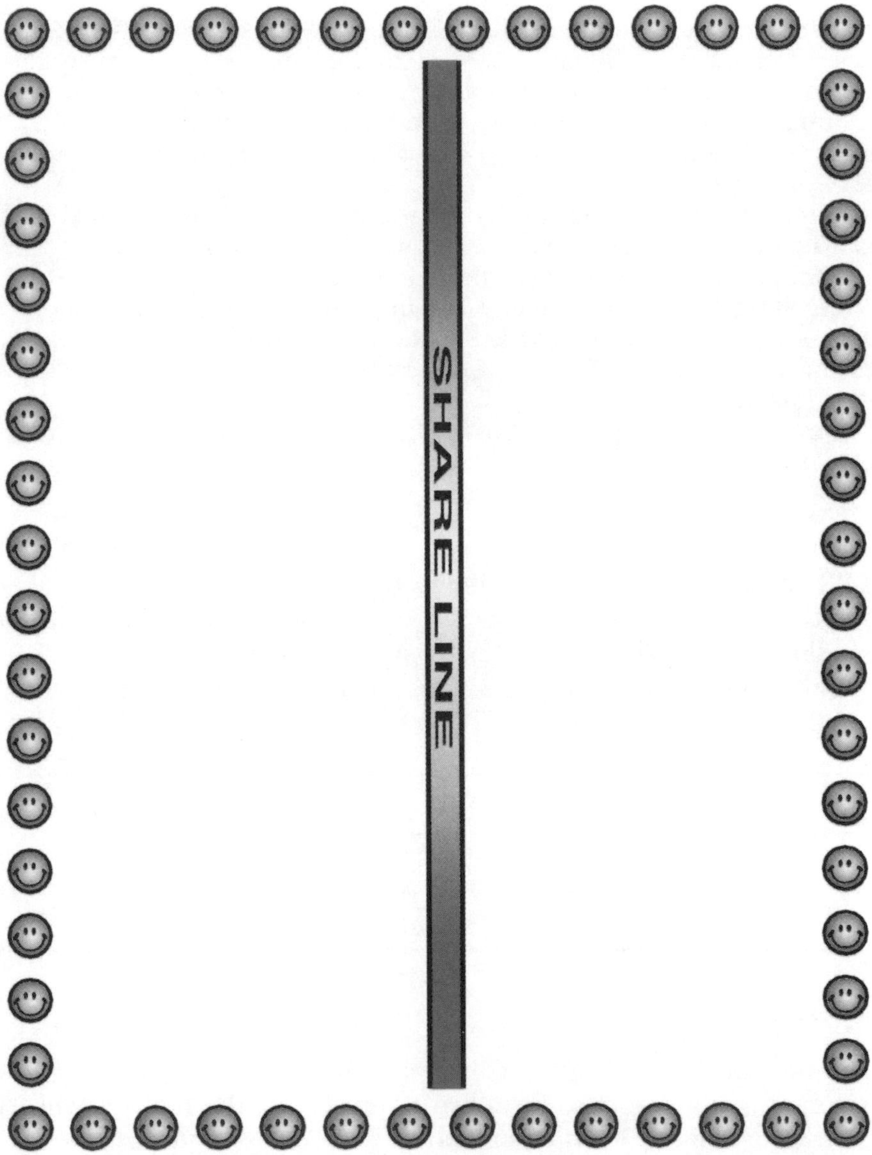

Anna

It is good to be in God's house.

I rejoiced with those who said to me, "Let us go to the house of the Lord."

Psalm 122:1

Anna Loved God's House

Dana was glad when her friend Deb said, "Let's go into the candy store and get a candy bar." Dana loved going to the candy store because the candy smelled so sweet. She could sit and smell it all day.

Anna, a woman in the Bible, loved a place with a sweet smell, God's house. God's house doesn't smell like a candy store, but it does smell sweet with God's love.

Anna was very old and in her eighties. Her husband had died when she was a young woman. She had been married only seven years when he died. Anna missed her husband, but knew God was with her.

She stayed at the temple day and night to pray and praise God because of His great love. She was there when Mary and Joseph had baby Jesus blessed at the temple. She was one of the first people to say, "God's Son, Jesus, has finally come."

Anna knew the importance of being in God's house. She knew that being there meant being in the presence of God's love.

Your Turn

1. Where are some places you like to go that are sweet to you?
2. Is there a place you like to visit because you know a certain person will be there? What about a farm where your grandparents are?
3. Who can you take with you to God's house next Sunday?

____

____

____

____

Prayer

Dear God, I'm glad I can go to Your house and be with my friends. I want to go to church more often so I can learn Your Word, the Bible. Thank You for all You have done so I can be in heaven with You someday. I thank You for dying on the cross to save me. Amen.

Candy Store Scramble

Read the words in the jars to see a message. Write the message on the sign in front of the store.

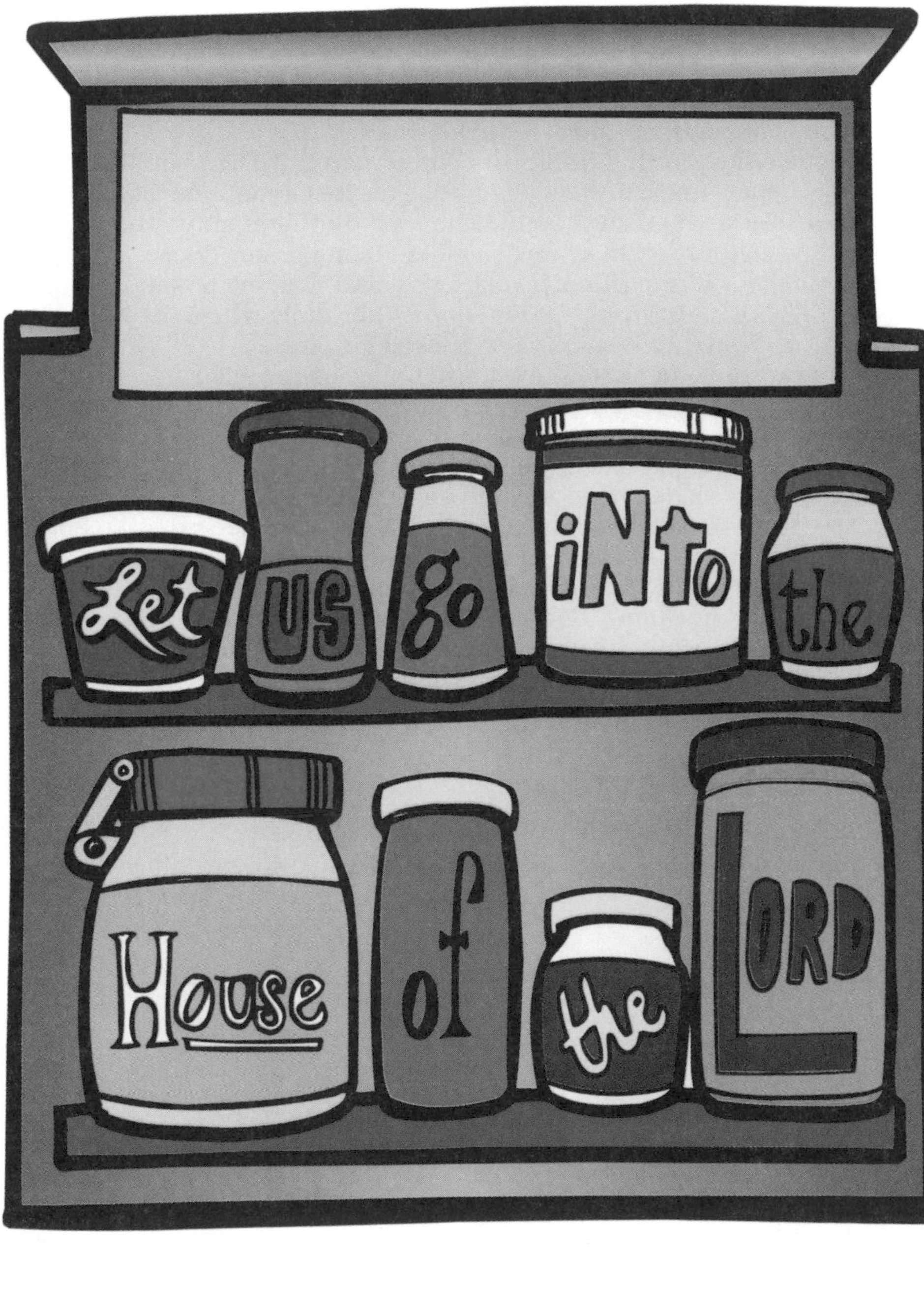

Anna

I love God's house.

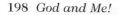

Blessed are those who dwell in your house.

Psalm 84:4

I Will Love God's House

Emily got an outdoor play house for her birthday. She spent every morning playing with her dolls in the house.

Emily had nine brothers and sisters in her family. Large families can be very noisy. Quiet times in the play house gave her time to be alone. There were other times when she loved having her brothers and sisters playing with her in the house. Either way, she liked being in her house.

One Sunday morning Emily woke early and ran out to the playhouse to see her dolls. She started to dress one of her dolls when she heard her mom's voice: "Emily, it's time to get dressed for church."

"I want to stay and play in my house today," she yelled.

Her mom walked over to a little window in the playhouse. "You love your house, don't you?" she asked Emily.

"Yes!" said Emily as she covered one of her dolls with a blanket.

Her mom stuck her head in the window. "God wants us to love His house, too," she said. "Sunday is called the Lord's day. We set aside Sunday as a special day to honor Him in His house, the church."

"I thought every day is God's day," said Emily.

"Well, it is," said Mom. "But part of loving God is going to His house on Sundays. Getting together with God's people pleases Him."

"My play house is nice, but I guess God's house is where I should be on Sundays," said Emily.

Your Turn

1. What is one way you can show God you love Him?
2. Which one is more important: going to God's house or doing what you want to do?

____

____

____

____

Prayer

Dear God, thank You for Your house. Teach me to love Your house more than any other things. Amen.

My Playhouse

The girl in the story wanted to spend time in the playhouse rather than go to church. What would you rather do than go to church? Write it down inside the playhouse below. Tell God you're sorry for putting your house ahead of His.

Lois and Eunice

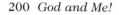

I can tell a Bible story to someone.

Do not be ashamed (uneasy) to testify about our Lord.

2 Timothy 1:8

Lois and Eunice Shared God's Word

Did you know that Abraham Lincoln went to school at home? He lived in the woods, far from a neighborhood school. His mother taught him well. She taught him science, history, math and the Bible. He grew up to be the 16th president of the United States.

The Bible tells about a boy named Timothy who was also schooled at home. Timothy's mother, Eunice, and his grandmother Lois were his teachers. They taught him the ways of God and the Bible.

The name Timothy means "one who honors God." Lois and Eunice taught him to honor God. These women were not too shy to tell Timothy about God. He grew up to be a pastor.

Timothy became a helper to Paul, the first missionary. He told others about Jesus' love for them and that He died for their sins.

Can you teach a Bible verse or Bible story to someone in your family? Do you have a little brother or sister whom you can help to learn God's Word? Teach them today! You never know, they may grow up to be a Lincoln or a Timothy. You may grow up to be a Lincoln or a Timothy, too! Pray for family members who haven't heard about Jesus.

Your Turn

1. Eunice and Lois passed on to Timothy their love for God. Do you know if your grandparents know God? Ask your mother and father if they were taught about God when they were little.
2. Where do you think Lois and Eunice learned about God?
3. When you grow up, if you have children do you think you should tell them about God?

____

____

____

____

Prayer

Dear God, I thank You that I can hear about You. I pray for the people in my family who don't know You. I pray they will hear that Jesus died for them and He wants to be their Lord and Savior. Amen.

Bible Teaching Plan

Pretend you are Lois or Eunice teaching Timothy about the Bible. Hand motions can help you learn a Bible verse. Learn the Bible verse below using hand motions and teach it to a brother, sister or cousin using the same hand motions. Make up your own hand motions to your favorite verses.

The Lord
Strength
Is My
and My Shield

Lois and Eunice

I can share God's word.

I am not ashamed (uneasy) of the gospel, because it is the power of God.

Romans 1:16

I Can Share God's Word

Girl testifies in robber's trial

A little girl told a judge that she saw a man in a mask running from a bank. The witness says she was coming from the library when she looked across the street and saw the man. She ran home and told her mother. Her mother called the police. The girl told police she was a little bit afraid, but that she would testify in the man's trial.

The girl in the newspaper story reported to police what she had seen. She may have felt a little uneasy telling what had happened. But she knew it was what God wanted her to do. The girl wasn't too shy to help police find the robber. Her news needed to be reported, so she reported it.

God's words in the Bible also need to be reported. The Bible won't help us find a robber, but it will help people find God. Sharing God's Word can help people live God's way.

The Old and New Testament in the Bible report the same things in different ways. God loved you so He sent His Son, Jesus, to die for your sins. Don't be afraid or too shy to tell others that the Bible is God's Word. Let people know that the Bible tells of God's power to help you live His way.

Your Turn

1. Why is the Bible a good news story?
2. What are God's words useful for?
3. Do you know people who need to hear about God's word? Who are they?

____

____

____

Prayer

Dear God, help me to read Your Word and tell others about the good news. Amen.

Verse Adventures

Write your favorite Bible verse on the magazine adventure page below. If you don't know a verse, use one from this book. Tell someone you know the verse and what it means.

Naaman's Servant Girl

I will try to do what is right.

Do what is right and good in the Lord's sight.

Deuteronomy 6:18

A Little Girl Does Right

Do you know when to do the right thing? It isn't always easy, is it?

A little girl from Israel did the right thing. The girl was taken away from her parents. The Bible says that she became a slave in the house of Naaman and his wife. Naaman was a mighty commander in the army of the king of Aram.

Naaman had a terrible skin illness. The little girl felt sorry for Naaman. She said to the commander's wife, "I wish Naaman would go to Elisha the prophet. He will heal him."

Naaman heard this and went to see Elisha. Elisha ordered Naaman to wash seven times in the Jordan River. At first Naaman was angry. Finally, he did what Elisha said to do. God healed him and he was very happy.

The little girl did the right thing by telling Naaman about God's prophet. The girl could have blamed Naaman that she had to be a slave. Instead, she did the right thing and helped her boss.

Your Turn

1. Why do you think the girl helped Naaman?
2. Is doing the right thing easy?
3. Would you have done the right thing if you were the girl?

____

____

____

____

____

____

____

____

Prayer

Lord, help me to do the right thing, even when it is hard. Amen.

Word Puzzle

The little girl did what was right to please God. Fill in the missing letters below. Review the verse to fill in the blanks. The answers are on page 232.

D_ w_a_ i_ r_g_t

_nd _oo_ _ _ t_ _

L_ _ _'s s_g_t.

Deuteronomy 6:18

Naaman's Servant Girl

I will keep doing the right thing.

And for you, brothers, never tire of doing what is right.

2 Thessalonians 3:13

I Can Do Right

The first time Linda played checkers with her brother, she lost. Every time she moved her checker to a square, he jumped over it with his checker. Then he took her checker. Pretty soon she had none left. Linda didn't make her checkers go to the right squares to escape being jumped.

Sometimes we are like Linda and the checkers game. We don't go where God wants us to go. Then we end up doing the wrong thing. Linda ended up on the wrong checker squares and you can, too.

Dina went to a candy store. She wished she had enough money to buy some candy, but she had no money. When she went into the store, the clerk was on the phone. Dina could have stolen the candy if she wanted to. It is like she was on a checker square ready to move. If she moved one way and walked out of the store, she would please God. If she moved a different way and stole the candy, she would do wrong. God wouldn't be pleased and she would get caught. Dina didn't take the candy. She moved on to the right square.

Your Turn

1. Why was it important for Linda to stay on the right square?
2. On what square does God want us to go?
3. Where does sin take us?

____

____

____

____

____

____

____

Prayer

Dear God, help me understand how to do right. Make me willing to follow the directions in the Bible. When I do wrong, put me back in the right square. Amen.

Checker Board Game

As long as Linda stayed on the right squares, she was OK. But when she moved her checker the wrong way, her brother jumped over it with his checker. Look at the board below. Move your checker to the squares that tell the right thing to do. Follow the arrows to the right squares.

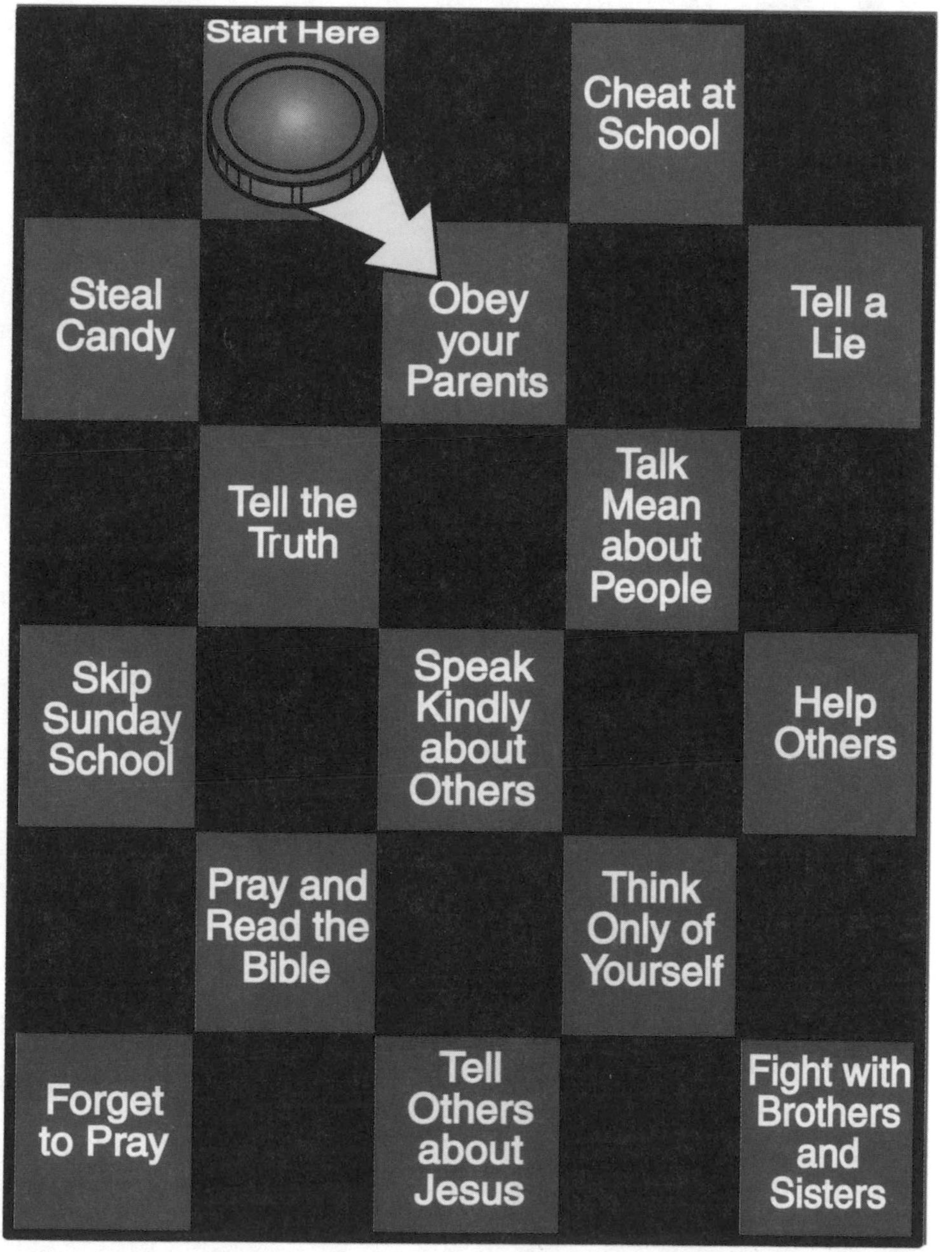

Who Am I?

Happy to Be Me

I am happy to be me.
You have filled my heart with greater joy.
Psalm 4:7

Being Happy Inside

"I made Mindy smile today, Mom," said Beth.

"How did you do that?" said Mom. "I know how sad she has been since her dad moved out. I guess her parents' divorce has been hard on her."

"Yes," said Beth. "I told her a knock-knock joke. It seemed to cheer her up."

Mom told Beth that her joke was a good idea. "That reminds me of a Bible verse," she said. "In Psalms, King David said, 'God has put gladness in my heart.' Then he said that the Lord will hear me when I call to Him."

"Does that mean that God made him happy by helping him?" asked Beth. "Yes!" said Mom. "When we know God loves us we are happy inside. In going through something sad like Mindy's problem, God's love helps. It's OK to be sad over problems. But, in times of problems, His love means more to us.'"

As Mindy's mom explained, only God can fill your heart with great joy. He even let His Son, Jesus, die for you on the cross. Jesus died to pay for your sins. That is the kind of love that should make you happy inside.

Your Turn

1. Why wasn't Mindy happy inside? Do you think she knew God wanted to help her?
2. How do you know God loves you?
3. How do you feel inside when you know God loves you?

____

____

____

____

____

Prayer

Dear God, You have put gladness in my heart. Help me to know Your love for me so I can be happy inside. Amen.

Jokes for God

Make up a knock-knock joke that can cheer someone and tell them about God at the same time. (Example: Knock, Knock. Who's there? Godso. Godso who? God so loved the world and you!)

Happy to Be Me

I am learning more about Jesus each day.
Grow in the...knowledge of our Lord.
2 Peter 3:18

Growing Each Day

Dee wanted to follow her older sister wherever she went.
"Please, can I go skating with you?" she would ask.
"No," her sister would say. "You're too little."
"Can I go to the movies with you?" asked Dee.
"No, you're too little."
"Can I go to the basketball game with you?"
"No, you're too little."
When will I ever grow up and do something fun? thought Dee.

Dee will grow up some day and so will you. You may be too little to do some things. But you are never too little to learn about Jesus and His love for you. That is called growing in the knowledge of Jesus. The Bible says you can always learn more about Jesus.

Jesus' friend Peter told us to grow in our love for Jesus. Faith is believing that God loves you. Faith is believing that He forgives your sins when you are sorry. Faith is believing that God wants you to be His child. That faith in Jesus and God can grow in you as you grow bigger.

Dee wanted to grow so she could follow her older sister. But Dee couldn't do what her sister was doing until she grows older. You can follow Jesus now.

Your Turn

1. What are some ways you keep learning more about Jesus?
2. How can your faith in God keep growing?
3. How do you plan to grow in knowing Jesus?

____

____

____

____

____

Prayer

Dear God, I want to keep growing as a follower of Jesus. Please help me to grow in faith by leading me to learn more about Jesus. Amen.

Growth Chart

Dee wanted to do everything her older sister was doing, but she was too little. Are there things you want to do, but are too little for? Jesus knows that you are too little to do some things. First He wants you to grow and learn. Then you can do things like go away to church camp. Look at the bottom of the growth chart. On lines one and two write two things you can do now. Look at the top of the growth chart. On lines three and four write two things you can do when you get older.

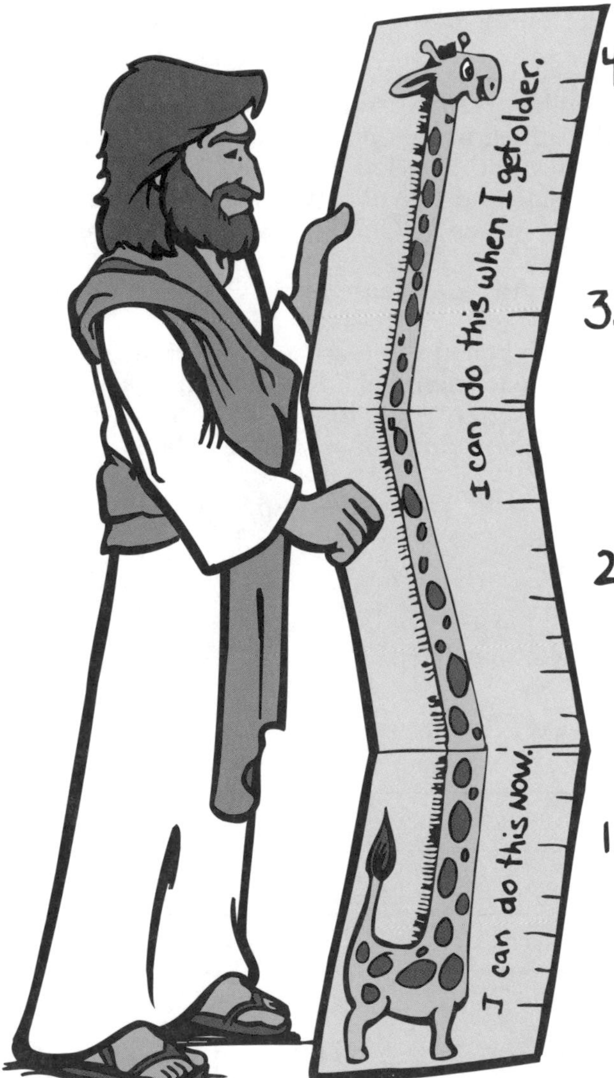

4. ____________________

3. ____________________

2. ____________________

1. ____________________

Happy to Be Me

I can trust God to not forget me.

The Lord is good...He cares for those who trust in him.

Nahum 1:7

God Never Forgets Me

The Huffs were on their way to Grandma's for the weekend. It got dark as they set out to drive the 200 miles to Grandma's farm. Pretty soon heavy rain fell. The rain fell so hard on the windshield of the car that Mr. Huff couldn't see the road in front of him. Soon they realized they were on the wrong road.

Mr. Huff said, "I guess the rain was so heavy that I missed my turn. Now we are lost." The Huffs' two children, Hope and Lora, began to cry.

"Are we really lost, Daddy? Lost means nobody knows where we are. We'll never get to Grandma's now!" they cried.

Mr. Huff pulled over to the side of the road to wait out the storm. "Yes, we will get to Grandma's house," he said. "God knows where we are. If we pray, He will help us find our way."

"Dear Father God," Mr. Huff prayed, "please help us find our way back to the main road."

Soon the family saw flashing lights in the rear view mirror of the car. It was a highway patrol officer. He lead them back to the main road.

Mr. Huff said, "See, kids, 'the Lord is good, He cares for those who trust Him.'" They made it to Grandma's in time for a bedtime snack. God had kept them safe and sound.

Don't be afraid to ask God for help. You are very special to Him. He will not forget you if you trust in Him.

Your Turn

1. What does God's Word say about trust?
2. Why can we trust God?
3. Do you think God would ever forget you?

____

____

____

____

Prayer

Dear God, I know You love me. You are a good God. I should trust You at all times. Sometimes I'm afraid. Forgive me and help me to trust that You won't forget me. Amen.

Raindrop Verse Scramble

Find the words in the Bible verse that are on the raindrops. Put them in the right order on the lines below the car. The answers are on page 232.

____ ____ ____   ____ ____ ____ ____
1 2 3   4 5 6 7

____ ____   ____ ____ ____ ____.
8 9   10 11 12 13

Happy to Be Me

I can do things with God's help.

I can do everything through him who gives me strength.

Philippians 4:13

I Can Be Strong

My daddy is the strongest man in the world, thought Abby.

Watching her father lift her little sister Lora up in the air was fun. Many times Abby also saw him lift heavy weights above his head.

"How strong are you, Daddy?" she asked. "Would you come to my room and move my desk? I can't do it. It's too heavy for me."

"Sure, I'll help you! We'll do it together," he said.

"After we move the desk, can you help me with my math paper?" asked Abby.

"Yes, honey, we can also do math together."

Abby's dad told her to put her hands on the desk. He stood behind her, placing his hands over hers. With his big hands on hers, they moved the desk together.

There are times when you need someone's help to do something like Abby did. God probably won't help you lift something but He will help you do things that make you who He wants you to be.

The Bible says you can do all things with Jesus' help. That doesn't mean that Jesus will help you do something wrong. Jesus will help you do what is good for you. With His help, you can be strong when you feel weak. All you need to do is ask Him.

Your Turn

1. Why couldn't Abby move the desk by herself?
2. What are some things you can't do by yourself?
3. Why is Jesus able to help you be strong when you feel weak?

Prayer

Dear Jesus, I know You are my friend and helper. I know that with Your help I can do anything You want me to. With Your help, I can be what You want me to be. Amen.

God's Hands

We are weak, but God is strong. Trace your hand on the x under God's hand. Let God be strong for you. On your hand, write down something with which you need God's help.

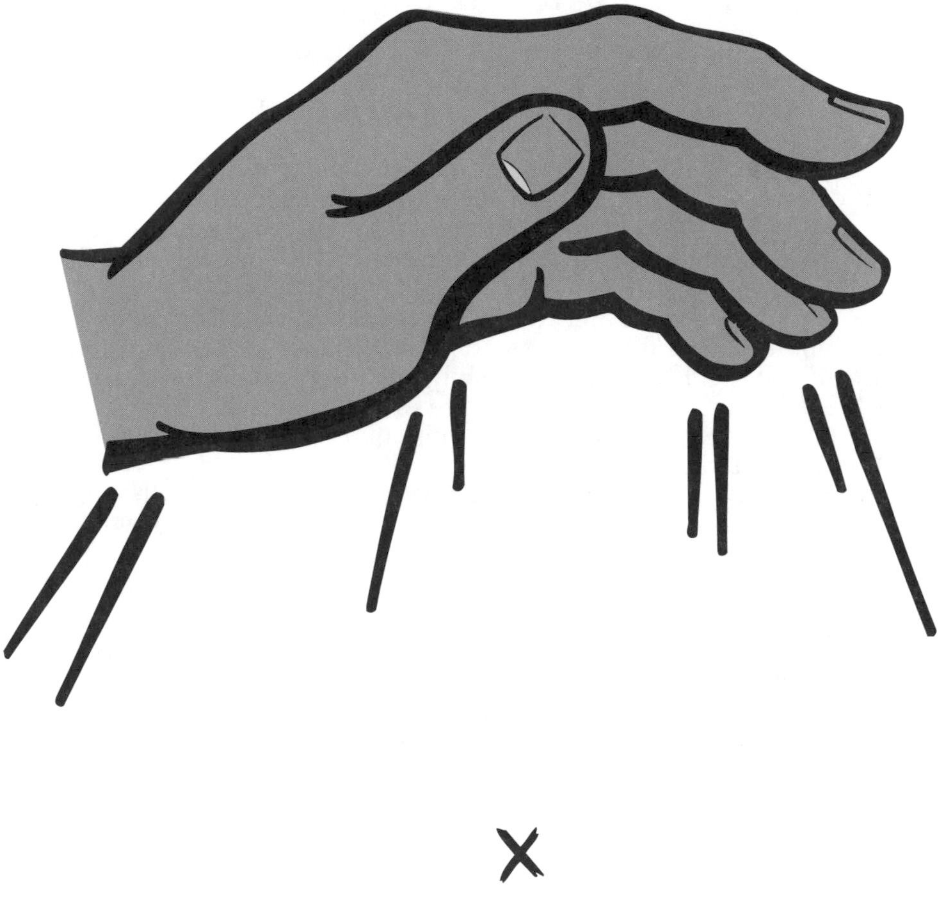

Happy to Be Me

I am fearfully made.

I praise you because I am fearfully and wonderfully made.

Psalm 139:14

Your Wonderful Body

Dory flipped through a stack of family pictures. Her baby pictures were always fun to look at.

"Look, Mom," said Dory. She held up her first baby picture. "See my little nose, Mom. Wasn't it cute?"

"It's still cute," said Mom. "You're just as wonderful today as you were the day you were born. Babies are such miracles. Dory, just look at your little feet, ears and fingers. God made you different than anyone else. See the little mole on your left big toe?" she asked. "Do you still have that on your toe?"

"Yes, it's still there. I think that was a mistake," said Dory.

"God doesn't make mistakes," said Mom. "He put that mole there. It is part of who you are. I can't think of anything more wonderfully made than our bodies."

"God must have something special planned for your life, Dory," Mom said. "Listen to Him to find out His plan for you."

Like Dory's mom said, you should always be happy with who you are. God doesn't make mistakes. You are perfect because He made you. Each of us is special in God's eyes.

Your Turn

1. Who made your body? Why?
2. What wonderful things have you noticed your body can do?
3. Are you happy with the way you look? Thank God for the way you look.

Prayer

Thank You, God, for my body. I am wonderfully made so I can serve You. Help me to take care of my body. Don't let me compare myself with others. Amen.

Wonderful Me Clips

God made you in a special way for a reason. Do you love who you are? God sure loves you the way you are. See the paper clipped to the clothespins below? Draw a picture of you when you were a baby on the first paper. On the second paper draw a picture of you today.

Happy to Be Me

I will be great for God.
Whoever wants to become great among you must be your servant.
Matthew 20:26

Being Great for God

The contest song, "There she is, Miss America," rang out as Kelly flipped on the TV. She plopped down in her bean bag to see the new contest winner.

"Look who got first place, Mom!" she said. "The second and third place winners look sad. I think they wanted to be first."

The newly-crowned Miss America spoke to the people. "I'm so surprised to have won," she said. "But I'm thankful to God that I have won. I want to give my life to serving God. I will use my mind to help God's people. The crown I wear is for God."

Some girls in the contest wanted to be first so they could be known by others. Their eyes were on themselves. The winner knew how to be great for God. She took her eyes off herself. She put her eyes on God.

I want to be like her, thought Kelly.

Your Turn

1. In what would you like to be first?
2. How does a person get to be first?
3. People try to be first without God. Does that please Him?

____

____

____

____

____

____

____

____

Prayer

Dear Lord Jesus, I'm glad I know You. Help me to keep my eyes on You. Let me do everything for You and not myself. Then I'll be first. Amen.

Great for God Crown

How will you be great for God? To be great for God you must be last to others. Write on the beauty contest crown the ways that God wants you to be first for Him.

Happy to Be Me

I should love my friends, even when they hurt me.
Bless those who curse you, pray for those who mistreat you.
Luke 6:28

Mean People and Me

"I don't like the girls next door. They are mean to me," said Megan. "I won't ever play with them again."

"What did they do?" asked Mom.

"They called me names. They don't ever ask me to play games with them. Even when I'm standing in front of them, they look the other way."

Mom listened carefully to Megan. Megan's story reminded her mother of her own childhood. A mean girl named Becky once threw her new shoes in the lake. *It's easy to feel hatred toward mean girls*, she thought.

"Megan, I know how you feel," she said. "The Bible says, 'Do good to those who hate you.' God wants us to love mean girls. He also wants us to forgive them." "That's too hard," said Megan.

"Maybe not!" said Mom. "What could you do for those girls, Megan?"

"I know!" said Megan. "I can offer to keep score for them in their game next time."

"Let's pray right now for the girls, Megan," said Mom.

Megan found ways to be nice to mean girls. It took a while, but the girls became friends with Megan. She even invited them to her Sunday school class. Once they heard about Jesus, they felt bad at how they had treated Megan.

Your Turn

1. How do mean girls or boys make you feel?
2. Do you feel better or worse when you are mean back?
3. Can you say the Bible verse that tells how to treat mean people?

____

____

____

____

____

____

Prayer

Dear Jesus, please help me love mean girls and boys. Help me not to be upset when they hurt me. Remind me to pray for them. Amen.

Wet Shoes

Megan's mother told how a mean girl had once thrown her shoes in the lake. Has anyone done something like that to you? Has anyone like Megan's neighbor been mean to you? Write down their names on the pair of shoes below. By writing down their names you are saying you want to forgive them. Now pray for them and ask God to help you forgive them.

Happy to Be Me

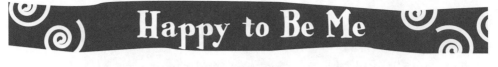

God wants what is best for me.
Yet not as I will, but as you will.
Matthew 26:39

The Best for Me

"You need to take your medicine." "Don't forget to wear a coat." "Put your bike helmet on." "Eat your peas."

Sometimes parents ask you to do things you don't understand. They want you to do things you don't like. But they have a reason for telling you to do something. If you love your parents, you will trust them to do what's best for you.

It's the same way with God. If you love God, you can trust Him to do what's best for you. If you love God you can say, "Not what I want God, but what You want."

Whatever God wants for you is always the best. God's love makes Him do what's best for you. God doesn't want anything to hurt you. Friends and family don't always obey God. They hurt others. Hurting others can stand in the way of God doing what's best for you. God always wants what is best. Can you help Him to do what's best for you and others?

Your Turn

1. Why should you let God decide things?
2. Why do you sometimes miss what's best for you?
3. What should you do to find out what's best for you?

____

____

____

____

____

____

____

____

Prayer

Dear God, help me to say You know what's best. When You tell me to do something, remind me that You know what's best for me. Amen.

Doing What's Best

Sometimes you don't want to do what your parents think is best. Under the medicine bottle with the happy face write three things that are best to do. (Example: Wash hands before eating.) Under the sad face write what's bad to do. (Example: Eat too much candy.)

Happy to Be Me

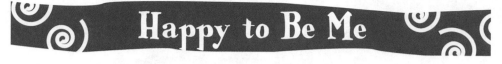

I show my love for God and Jesus.
I will show you my faith by what I do.
James 2:18

What I Believe

Jamie said she believes in Jesus and loves Him.

But...she got into a fight with her brother and hit him with the fireplace poker. He had 10 stitches.

Then...Jamie told her parents she didn't have to obey them.

Then...her teacher sent her to the office because she wouldn't obey at school. Jamie carries anger in her heart for other kids at school.

That Sunday at church, the children's pastor asked Jamie if she was a Christian. Jamie said, "Of course I'm a Christian. I go to church, don't I? Surely you can see that I'm a Christian."

But was Jamie following Christ? Is getting sent to the school office a way to show others you are a Christian? Christians are people who love Jesus and want to follow Him. They want Jesus to be Savior and Lord in their life. Christians like the things Jesus likes. They trust Jesus to help them do things God's way. That is also called faith.

How do you show others your faith? How do people know you are a Christian? Jamie said she was a Christian. She didn't act like she wanted to obey God. One way to show faith in Jesus is to obey God.

Your Turn

1. What is faith in Jesus?
2. How do you show people you are a true follower of Jesus?

____

____

____

____

____

____

Prayer

Dear God, forgive me for not showing others I believe in You. Help me to show my faith in You by obeying. Amen.

What I Believe

Following Jesus is like being a shadow of Jesus. Make a list of the ways you show you follow Jesus. How can people know that you love Jesus?

Happy to Be Me

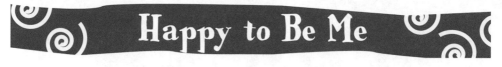

God can clean my heart.
Wash me, and I will be whiter than snow.
Psalm 51:7

Being Clean Inside

"How did your new white tennis shoes get mud on them?" Mom asked Monica. "Look at the mud spots on your white shoes."

"I stepped in a mud puddle at recess today," said Monica.

"I guess I'll have to put them in the washing machine with bleach," said Mom. "Monica, I can tell it's going to be hard to keep those shoes clean. But no matter how many times those shoes get dirty, we should be able to clean them with bleach."

Bleach can't wash away the bad things you say and do. It can't wash a person's sins away. Only God can do that. When God forgives your wrongdoing, it is washed away.

King David asked God to wash Him so He could be whiter than snow. When you do wrong, it is sin. Sin is like the mud spots on Monica's shoes. God doesn't care if your shoes are clean. He wants His people to be clean on the inside.

A girl who is clean on the inside is pleasing to God. Would you like a clean heart inside? Be sorry for doing wrong and ask God to forgive you. He will forgive and make you white as snow.

Your Turn

1. Could Monica's mom wash Monica's shoes and heart?
2. How many sins can God wash? Are there any sins that can't be washed away?
3. How does God wash your sins away?

____

____

____

____

____

____

Prayer

Dear God, forgive me for my sins (name some of your recent sins). I want to be made whiter than snow. Amen.

Monica's Shoe Maze

Color white each of Monica's shoes that shows sin as they lead to a clean heart. Only Jesus can wash your heart clean.

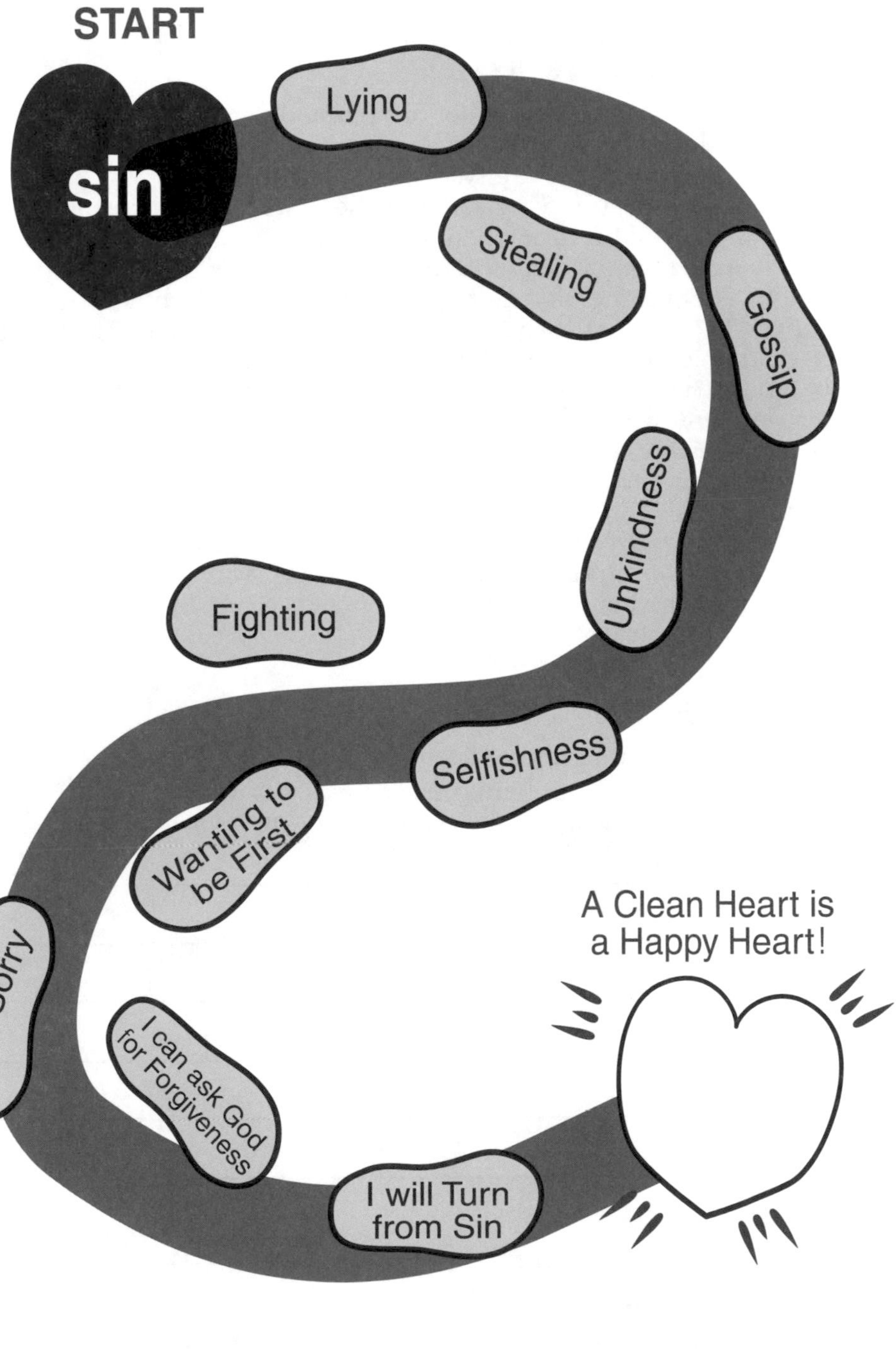

Happy to Be Me

I will be ready for You, Jesus.

You also must be ready, because the Son of Man will come.

Luke 12:40

I'm Ready for Jesus

Wendy lived on a farm with her brother and parents. One day her father said he would need to go away for a while. Their farm would be taken away if he didn't go to work in the city.

At first, Wendy was very sad that her father was leaving. Then her father said he would return when he had money to save the farm. He also said he loved her and wouldn't forget her.

Wendy, her brother and mother worked very hard while Wendy's father was gone. They got up early to milk cows and feed chickens. Her brother plowed and planted the field. Life would have problems and be hard until their father came home. But they were happy because they knew their father would return.

That's the way it is with Jesus. Living here on earth is hard work for a while. You may have problems and sadness. But, Jesus has promised He will return to this earth someday. Jesus loves you and wants you to be with Him in heaven. But you can be happy and cheerful now. God doesn't want you to worry or be afraid of Jesus coming again. You are loved by God and you will be safe when Jesus comes again. Be ready by loving others and working hard for Jesus.

Your Turn

1. How can you be ready for Jesus' return?
2. What keeps you from being ready for Jesus' return?
3. Should you be afraid of Jesus coming again?

Prayer

Jesus, help me to be ready for You to come again. Help me to love You and serve You while I wait. Amen.

Seed Planting

Get ready for Jesus' coming by doing things that please Him. Write under the stalks things that you can do.

_______________ _______________ _______________

Answers

p. 31: top left with bottom right; second on left with third on right; third on left with top on right; bottom on left with second on right

p. 43: You remain the same, God.

p. 47: The right arm, left eye, left ear, right leg and part of the right ear are missing.

p. 97:

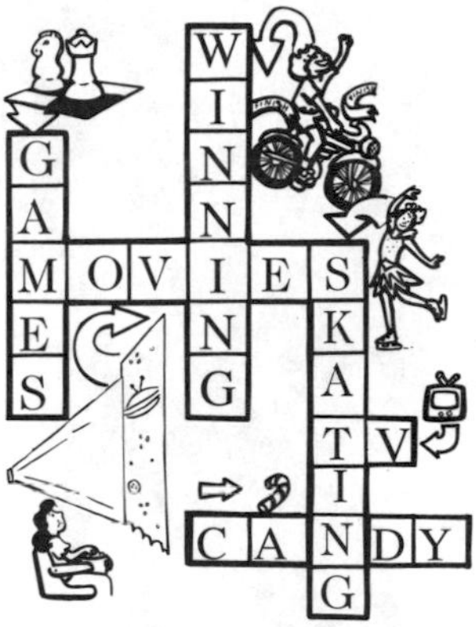

p. 99: I will put God first.

p. 117: first, most, name, Sundays, father, mother, life, marry, yours, yours, honest

p. 131:

p. 137: Be strong and courageous. Deuteronomy 31:7

P. 149:

Q	R	K	W	I	J
S	L	M	H	M	E
Z	F	P	A	Z	S
W	U	O	T	O	U
W	O	U	L	D	S

p. 157:

p. 167: Praise the Lord for He is good.

p. 175: I love my Jesus.

p. 187: Let us not become weary of doing good.

p. 205: Do what is right and good in the Lord's sight.

p. 215: The Lord is good.